santa REMEMBERED

Representing the best that is in all of us, Santa Claus helps fill our timeless need to have something good to believe in. With his love, compassion, and selfless giving, this plump and jolly man helps us retain a sense of childlike wonder. As we celebrate Christmas, he seems to be everywhere at once, radiating a warmth that inspires us to be more like him.

Whether we know him as Santa Claus, Weihnachtsmann, Father Christmas, or some other holiday figure, our memories of this childhood friend are treasured, stored, and occasionally taken out to be shared. Each year as we pass around the Christmas punch, trim the tree, and exchange gifts, we always, in some way, remember Santa Claus.

Join us now as we look back through the eyes of turn-of-the-century artists at some earlier images of this beloved man. Come along as we retrace his steps through the years and discover his rich, age-old English and European heritage.

The portraits included in this nostalgic journey were lovingly adapted for cross stitch from 22 antique postcards. As you read the stories and stitch the designs, we hope you'll experience the joy that remembering Santa brings!

LEISURE ARTS, INC.
Little Rock, Arkansas

International Standard Book Number 0-942237-05-6

Santa Claus hasn't always looked like the jolly old fellow we know today. Like so many other American traditions, he's a product of the great American melting pot — a blending of many different cultures and customs. His earliest ancestors date back to pre-Christian days, when sky-riding gods ruled the earth. The mythological characters Odin, Thor, and Saturn gave us the basis for many of Santa's distinctive characteristics.

But the most influential figure in the shaping of today's generous and loving Santa Claus was a real man, St. Nicholas of Myra (now Turkey), a fourth century bishop. As a champion of children and the needy, he was legendary for his kindness and generosity.

A TRADITION OF BENEVOLENCE

In a well-known story illustrating St. Nicholas' benevolence, we find two of the basic principles of the holiday spirit — giving to others and helping the less fortunate — as well as the tradition of hanging stockings by the fireplace.

According to this legend, there were three Italian maidens whose family had fallen on hard times. Because their father couldn't afford the dowries necessary for them to marry, he was considering selling one of his daughters into slavery to get dowries for the other two. When the good saint heard of the family's plight, he went to their home late one night and anonymously tossed three bags of gold down the chimney. Miraculously, a bag fell into each of the sisters' stockings, which were hanging by the fire to dry. His kindhearted gift made it possible for all three maidens to marry.

A variation of this story is that as each girl was ready to wed, St. Nicholas came in the middle of the night when no one could see him and tossed a bag of gold through an open window into her stocking. This idea of gifts being delivered through an open window may have begun as a way to explain how Santa enters homes that have no chimney.

PATRON SAINT

Because of his wisdom and sensitivity, many groups claimed St. Nicholas as their patron saint. Children, orphans, sailors, and even thieves often prayed to the compassionate saint for guidance and protection. Entire countries, including Russia and Greece, also adopted him as their patron saint, as well as students and pawnbrokers.

Throughout his life, St. Nicholas tried to help others while also inspiring them to imitate his virtues. Legends of his unselfish giving spread all over northern Europe, and accounts of his heroic deeds blended with regional folklore. Eventually, the image of the stately saint was transformed into an almost mystical being, one known for rewarding the good and punishing the bad.

he date of his death, December 6th, was commemorated with an annual feast, which gradually came to mark the beginning of the medieval Christmas season. On St. Nicholas' Eve, youngsters would set out food for the saint, straw for his horse, and schnapps for his attendant. The next morning, obedient children awoke to find their gifts replaced with sweets and toys, but naughty ones found their offerings untouched, along with a rod or bundle of switches. St. Nicholas' Day is still observed in many countries, and gifts are exchanged in honor of the spirit of brotherhood and charity that he embodied.

THE MAKING OF SANTA CLAUS

After the Protestant Reformation in the sixteenth century, the feasting and veneration of Catholic saints were banned. But people had become accustomed to the annual visit from their gift-giving saint and didn't want to forget the purpose of the holiday. So in some countries, the festivities of St. Nicholas' Day were merged with Christmas celebrations, and although the gift-bearer took on new, nonreligious forms, he still reflected the saint's generous spirit.

In Germany, he appeared as Weihnachtsmann, in England as Father Christmas, and in France, as Père Noël, who left small gifts in the children's shoes.

In the areas where St. Nicholas was still portrayed as the gift-bringer, a host of other characters developed as his assistants. Two of his most well-known helpers were Knecht Ruprecht and the Belsnickel. Depending on the local tradition, they were either attendants to St. Nicholas or gift-bearers themselves, but in all cases, both were fearsome characters, brandishing rods or switches. It was their duty not only to reward good children but also to reprove children who were naughty or couldn't recite their prayers.

Knecht Ruprecht (meaning Servant Rupert) was also known by other names such as Black Peter (so called because he delivered the presents down the chimney for St. Nicholas and became blackened with soot).

In some places, the images of Knecht Ruprecht and St. Nicholas merged to form Ru Klaus (meaning Rough Nicholas — so named because of his rugged appearance), Aschen Klaus (meaning Ash Nicholas — because he carried a sack of ashes as well as a bundle of switches), and Pelznickel (meaning Furry Nicholas — referring to his fur-clad appearance).

When the Germans settled Pennsylvania in the eighteenth century, they brought stories of the Belsnickel. With his Old World custom of meting out rewards and punishments, he frightened even the most well-behaved children, yet his yearly visit was eagerly anticipated.

Not all of St. Nicholas' companions were frightening. In fact, the Christkindl (meaning Christ Child) was thought to accompany him in many countries. Often portrayed by a fair-haired young girl, this angelic figure was sometimes the gift-bearer, too.

SANTA IN AMERICA

 mmigrants to the New World brought along their various beliefs when they crossed the Atlantic. The Scandinavians introduced gift-giving elves, the Germans brought not only their Belsnickel and Christkindl but also their decorated trees, and the Irish contributed the ancient Gaelic custom of placing a lighted candle in the window.

In the 1600's, the Dutch presented Sinterklaas (meaning St. Nicholas) to the colonies. In their excitement, many English-speaking children uttered the name so quickly that Sinterklaas sounded like Santy Claus. After years of mispronunciation, the name evolved into Santa Claus.

In 1808, American author Washington Irving created a new version of old St. Nick. This one rode over the treetops in a horse-drawn wagon "dropping gifts down the chimneys of his favorites." In his satire, *Diedrich Knickerbocker's History of New York from the Beginning of the World to the End of the Dutch Dynasty,* Irving described Santa as a jolly Dutchman who smoked a long-stemmed clay pipe and wore baggy breeches and a broad-brimmed hat. Also, the familiar phrase, "...laying his finger beside his nose...," first appeared in Irving's story.

That phrase was used again in 1822 in the now-classic poem by Dr. Clement Clarke Moore, "A Visit from St. Nicholas," more commonly known as "The Night Before Christmas." His verse gave an Arctic flavor to Santa's image when he substituted eight tiny reindeer and a sleigh for Irving's horse and wagon. It is Moore's description of Santa that we most often think of today: "He had a broad face, and a little round belly, that shook, when he laughed, like a bowl full of jelly."

Up to this point, Santa's physical appearance and the color of his suit were open to individual interpretation. Then in 1863, Thomas Nast, a German immigrant, gave us a visual image of the cheerful giver that was to later become widely accepted.

When Nast was asked to illustrate Moore's charming verse for a book of children's poems, he gave us a softer, kinder Santa who was still old but appeared less stern than the ecclesiastical St. Nicholas. He dressed his elfin figure in red and endowed him with human characteristics. Most important of all, Nast gave Santa a home at the North Pole. For twenty-three years, his annual drawings for *Harper's Weekly* magazine allowed Americans to peek into the magical world of Santa Claus and set the stage for the shaping of today's merry gentleman.

Artist Haddon Sundblom added the final touches to Santa's modern image. Beginning in 1931, his billboards and other advertisements for Coca-Cola® featured a portly, grandfatherly Santa with human proportions and a ruddy complexion. Sundblom's exuberant, twinkling-eyed Santa firmly fixed the gift-giver's image in the public mind.

St. Nicholas' evolution into today's happy, larger-than-life Santa Claus is a wonderful example of the blending of countless beliefs and practices from around the world. This benevolent figure encompasses all the goodness and innocence of childhood. And because goodness is his very essence, in every kindness we do, Santa will always be remembered.

TABLE OF CONTENTS

EDITORIAL STAFF — EDITOR-IN-CHIEF: Anne Van Wagner Young. MANAGING EDITOR: Sandra Graham Case. CREATIVE ART DIRECTOR: Gloria Hodgson. ASSISTANT EDITOR: Susan Frantz Wiles. PRODUCTION DIRECTORS: Carla Bentley and Jana Berryman. PRODUCTION ASSISTANTS: Ginger Alumbaugh, Lisa Arey, Kandi Ashford, Kay Beasley, Kathy Bradley, Carolyn Breeding, Jane Chandler, Teal Elliott, Lisa Hinkle, Susan McGee, Candy Murphy, Pam Necessary, Debra Smith, Christine Street, Amy Taylor, Shannon Wells, Janet Yearby, and Pam Young. EDITORIAL DIRECTOR: Dorothy Latimer Johnson. EDITORIAL ASSISTANT: Tammi Foress Williamson. COPY ASSISTANTS: Linda L. Trimble, Marjorie Lacy Bishop, Tena Kelley Vaughn, and Darla Burdette Kelsay. PRODUCTION ART DIRECTOR: Melinda Stout. CREATIVE ART ASSISTANT: Linda Lovette. PRODUCTION ART SUPERVISOR: Jeff Curtis. PRODUCTION ARTISTS: Roberta Aulwes, Don Brown, Pat Farmer, Rhonda Hodge, Leslie Loring Krebs, Martha Marx, Kermit Payne, Eric Pipkin, Mike Spigner, Andy Warren, Tony Wickliffe, Karen Wilson, and Jennifer Young. PHOTO STYLIST: Karen Smart Hall. TYPESETTERS: Laura Glover Burris and Vicky Fielder Johnson.

BUSINESS STAFF — PUBLISHER: Steve Patterson. CONTROLLER: Tom Siebenmorgen. RETAIL SALES DIRECTOR: Richard Tignor. RETAIL MARKETING DIRECTOR: Pam Stebbins. RETAIL CUSTOMER SERVICES DIRECTOR: Margaret Sweetin. MARKETING MANAGER: Russ Barnett. CIRCULATION MANAGER: Guy A. Crossley. PRINT PRODUCTION MANAGER: Chris Schaefer.

CREDITS — NEEDLEWORK ADAPTATIONS: Carol Emmer. PHOTOGRAPHY: Mark Mathews (cover) and Ken West (projects) of Peerless Photography, Little Rock, Arkansas. COLOR SEPARATIONS: Magna IV Engravers, Little Rock, Arkansas.

MERRY OLDE GENT

Smiling eyes, a soft white beard, and a fur-trimmed cap — this is the Santa we know today. A wonderful blend of timeless features, this image has been created for us by generations of devoted Santa Claus enthusiasts.

It was Dr. Clement Clarke Moore who put the twinkle in Santa's eyes with his 1822 poem, "The Night Before Christmas." In creating his plump, cheerful image of St. Nick, Moore drew from ancient legends as well as contemporary tales. Some researchers also report a real-life influence on Moore's portrait of Santa — Jan Duyckinck, his caretaker. A jovial, portly Dutchman, Jan sported a white beard and was fond of smoking a pipe.

Since the poem was introduced so many Christmas Eves ago, the American image of Santa Claus has been molded by countless artists and storytellers. As you turn the pages of this book, you'll see many of the historical images that contributed to our modern Santa, from an ornately robed bishop to a humble saint and an elfin Kris Kringle. One portrait even shows Santa in all-American red, white, and blue. A little part of each of these figures lives on in the Santa we know and love today.

I WISH YOU A MERRY CHRISTMAS

O, STARRY NIGHT

Perhaps because the Star of Bethlehem guided the Magi to the Christ Child, stars have taken on a special significance in the Christmas story.

In this handsome piece, the dazzling array of stars on the old gentleman's robe are reminiscent of that heavenly light. The star has also come to represent Christ, who was called the Bright and Morning Star.

For many, placing a lighted star atop the Christmas tree has become a cherished holiday tradition. And in some parts of the world, the celebration begins with the sighting of the first star of Christmas Eve.

And, lo, the star, which they saw in the east, went before them, till it came and stood over where the young Child was.

— MATTHEW 2:9

A MERRY CHRISTMAS

making a list

the belief that Santa keeps a list of who's been naughty and who's been nice magically transforms even the most unruly youngsters into angels. Some say he also maintains a list to keep up with all the mail he gets from children during the holiday season.

In Bavaria and Austria, however, Christmas wish lists are traditionally addressed to "Dear Jesus in Heaven." The letters are placed on the windowsills for St. Nicholas to pick up on December 5, the eve of his feast day. The good saint then takes the letters to the Christ Child, who delivers the gifts on Christmas Eve.

The charcoal color of this somber gentleman's robe is in keeping with the religious note of St. Nicholas' early appearance.

weihnachtsmann

In this wintry scene, the colorfully robed German Weihnachtsmann (meaning Christmas Man) leaves a little village and heads for his next destination. Some Europeans believe he is sent by the Christkindl (Christ Child) to deliver gifts on Christmas Eve.

While traveling on foot, the humble old gentleman carries an evergreen in one hand and switches for unruly children in the other. Toys and other goodies are tucked safely in packs on his back.

This secular figure developed after the Reformation when the feast and veneration of St. Nicholas was abolished in many countries.

A MERRY CHRISTMAS

gentle st. nick

Compassionate eyes and a softly knitted brow express the benevolence that generations have attributed to St. Nicholas. Cloaked in rich shades of red and surrounded by lush greenery, this kindly saint glows in the warmth of traditional holiday colors.

He wears the color of charity, red, which also symbolizes the blood of Christ. The vibrant crimson and scarlet hues are so flawlessly blended you can almost feel the robe's texture with your eyes.

Sprigs of evergreen, signifying the hope for eternal life, and a sprinkling of snowy white for purity complete the setting for the gentle St. Nick.

memorable stroll

A merry Christmas.

Oh, the lucky children who could enjoy a stroll with Santa! Many youngsters today would cherish such a special moment. However, because Santa is so busy checking his lists and making toys, they have to settle for a brief visit with him at their local department store. Often standing in line behind countless others, excited children eagerly wait for the chance to climb onto Santa's lap and whisper their hearts' desires into his ear.

In part, the tradition of visiting with a department store Santa Claus goes back to the 1400's. Schoolmasters in those days would often impersonate the good saint at school celebrations on St. Nicholas' Day. They donned red robes and long white beards and talked with students individually. After urging the pupils to be obedient and to study hard, "St. Nicholas" gave them small gifts such as apples, nuts, and pens.

CHRISTMAS RIDER

In his jewel-tone coat and whimsical shoes, this Santa has chosen to travel atop a sure-footed little donkey. Today we're so accustomed to seeing Santa in a sleigh drawn by eight reindeer that it's difficult to imagine him traveling any other way. But through the years, he has used whatever means were available — even a wagon pulled by a team of goats or horses — to complete his joyful mission.

In many Latin American countries, the donkey, which is a familiar mode of transportation, often brings Balthazar, one of the Three Wise Men, instead of Santa. Balthazar and the other Magi, Caspar and Melchior, are believed to come on January 5th, the eve of Epiphany, to fill the children's shoes with gifts.

The little burro in this portrait also reminds us of the donkey that Mary rode to Bethlehem just before the birth of Jesus. This blending of religious and secular images was common in earlier times.

TRAVELING COMPANIONS

Christmas Greetings

turn-of-the-century artists often painted Santa Claus wearing colors other than red, but it was rare to see him dressed in a yellow robe such as this one. It was also unusual for artists of that time to portray the Christmas caller with reindeer, although today no Santa Claus story would be complete without these magical companions.

An old sailor's legend helps explain why we believe Santa travels through the sky on Christmas Eve. In this story, a ship had run aground during a terrible storm. The captain and crew prayed to St. Nicholas, the patron saint of sailors, to save them from certain death. All at once the saint appeared, flying down from the clouds toward the helpless sailors. He prayed with the men and helped them free their ship. Then without another word, he was gone as suddenly as he had appeared.

Another influence on Santa's heavenly mode of travel was the Norse god Thor, who rode across the sky in a chariot drawn by two white goats, Gnasher and Cracker.

Dr. Clement Clarke Moore used these ideas in his 1822 holiday poem, "The Night Before Christmas," which featured eight reindeer drawing Santa's sleigh. This beloved tale won a place in American Christmas history for Dasher, Dancer, Prancer, Vixen, Comet, Cupid, Donder, and Blitzen.

father Christmas

ere the magic and excitement of the holiday season radiate from the faces of Father Christmas and an enthusiastic child. Originating in England, this jovial giant symbolizes the feasting and merriment of midwinter celebrations.

He is usually portrayed as a heavily bearded, friendly fellow wearing a crown of holly and a scarlet or green fur-lined robe. Often, he carries the Yule log and a bowl of Christmas punch.

For many, his prickly crown of holly represents the crown of thorns that Jesus wore when He was crucified, and the red berries are symbolic of the blood He shed.

Of all the nighttime gift-givers, Father Christmas has perhaps the strongest ties to pre-Christian gods. This jolly fellow is a blending of the Roman god Saturn, who came bearing food, wine, joy, and revelry; the Scandinavian god Odin, who brought reward and punishment; and Odin's son Thor, who rode through the skies in a chariot drawn by a team of goats.

Christmas Greetings

EVER GREEN, EVER GIVING

Whether bare or decorated with bright and shiny ornaments, the evergreen tree is one of the most widely recognized symbols of the holiday season. In some areas, the family gathers to trim the Christmas tree; in others, Santa delivers the tree when he brings the presents.

The role of the evergreen in midwinter celebrations dates back to pre-Christian times when the tree symbolized nature's triumph over winter's darkness and deathly cold.

Christians began using evergreens as a reminder of Christ's gift of everlasting life. An eighth century Christian missionary is credited with originating the use of evergreens as Christmas trees. One Christmas Eve, as the German legend goes, St. Boniface came upon a group of pagan worshipers gathered about a giant oak to sacrifice a child to their god, Thor. To stop the murder, the saint toppled the mighty tree with one blow of his ax, and a tiny fir tree sprang up in its place.

Amazed by what had happened, the group asked St. Boniface to share God's Word. The blessed saint told them that the little fir was the Tree of Life and that it represented the eternal life of Christ, who was a bringer of life "ever green."

Since this miracle in the woods, the tree has become an indispensable part of the holiday celebration.

A MERRY CHRISTMAS

patron saint of children

Clad in traditional bishop's robes, this stately figure exemplifies the special relationship St. Nicholas is said to have enjoyed with children. Known for his great love for them, the good saint would often lead groups of youngsters in Bible study and afterward present them with small gifts as tokens of his affection.

It was said that even as an infant, St. Nicholas was both physically and spiritually precocious, displaying such reverent behavior as refusing food on fast days and doing wondrous works on behalf of children. Because he was orphaned at a young age, the kind saint shared an extra special bond with parentless children and became their protector.

One of the most enduring legends that helped establish St. Nicholas as the patron saint of little ones involves the rescue of a boy named Basilios. He was kidnapped by pirates on St. Nicholas' Day (December 6) and taken to Crete to be a slave. As the following December 6 approached, his family was saddened by the memory of their loss. In answer to their prayers for the boy's safe return, the good saint carried Basilios through the air back to his home. Then the thankful family once again observed St. Nicholas' Day as a time of celebration.

A Merry Christmas.

RINGING IN CHRISTMAS

A Merry Christmas

Early depictions of Kris Kringle showed him in long brown robes such as this one. Through the years, his dress changed to reflect changing fashions, and in many countries, he lost his somber ecclesiastical appearance. Today, Santa Claus is most often portrayed in a cheery, bright red suit.

A blending of the German gift-bearers Christkindl and Belsnickel, Kris Kringle is very similar to our modern-day Santa Claus in that he, too, is a holiday gift-bringer. However, unlike Santa, he rings a bell to signal that he has delivered his presents.

In some European countries, it's the Child Jesus whose holiday visit is proclaimed by the tinkling sound of chimes. Children believe He helps their parents prepare the tree and lay out gifts. When He has finished, a bell rings to signal His departure. Then the eager youngsters enter the room and enjoy their Christmas goodies.

BRINGING CHRISTMAS SPIRIT

a symbol of life in the bleak chill of winter, greenery adds as much to the joy of Christmas as toys, and this holiday traveler is prepared to deliver both. Mistletoe and holly, like that overflowing from his baskets, have been used for decorations since pre-Christian times.

The appearance of the flaming red holly berries opened the season of feasting and good cheer in old England. In Europe, it was believed that the first of two kinds of holly — the prickly "he" or the smooth "she" — brought into the home at Christmas determined whether the husband or wife would rule during the coming year.

The tradition of kissing under the mistletoe began with the Norse goddess Frigga. When her son, Balder, was killed by an arrow made of mistletoe, she wept tears of white berries and brought him back to life. Overjoyed, Frigga blessed the plant and promised to kiss all who passed beneath it.

In ancient Britain, mistletoe was so sacred that enemies meeting beneath a bough would put aside their arms, greet each other as friends, and observe a truce until the next day.

Though we no longer hold the old superstitions, these ancient customs still flavor our celebrations today. Nearly everyone enjoys the beauty of evergreens — and the fun of catching someone beneath the mistletoe.

grandfatherly gent

Early depictions of Santa often showed him as an elderly gentleman, without the softness and playful look of today's merry old elf. The stern appearance of these older portraits may reflect the influence of St. Nicholas, who was usually shown as a stately and somewhat grandfatherly man.

And yet this paternal image seems appropriate for the gift-giving benefactor, who was fond of bestowing fruits, nuts, and other little tokens of affection upon children after a Bible lesson.

Today, as in St. Nicholas' time, these treats are commonly given as small gifts. And in many homes, fruits and nuts have become traditional decorations.

a splendid sight

Fröhliche Weihnachten.

Just a glimpse of Santa's scarlet coat and his bright holiday trappings is enough to send young hearts racing. As these two little ones spot the holiday caller, they surely must wonder what Christmas surprises the jolly gent carries in his pack.

Santa's red robe is a reminder of the ecclesiastical robes of St. Nicholas, and the ornate design of this one reflects the lavish Victorian style that was prevalent at the turn of the century. Also popular during this time was the use of opulent, brightly colored ornaments such as those on the Christmas tree he is carrying.

The German custom of trimming an evergreen at Christmas became even more popular in England when Queen Victoria married Prince Albert of Germany. At first, the evergreen was adorned with candles, glass balls, and tinsel. Later foil-wrapped nuts, candied fruits, and cookies shaped like angels and stars were added to its branches. Noted for their love of elaborate decorations, Victorian ladies designed intricate paper and needlework ornaments to embellish their trees.

From the time ornaments were first added to an evergreen, decorating the Christmas tree has become an art form in its own right. Today it is a beloved holiday tradition shared by families and communities all over the world.

miles to go

the mystery of how Santa makes his whirlwind trip around the world in one night has fascinated children for generations. But young, active imaginations have always come up with creative answers.

Actually, with so many stops to make in such a short time, sometimes even an experienced world traveler like Santa Claus surely has to pause and check his directions. Yet somehow, year after year, through the dark of night, this merry Christmas visitor completes his joyful journey.

A happy CHRISTMAS.

santa's helper

finding out who's been naughty and nice is a monumental task, and many children have been told that Santa Claus must surely have some trusted helpers to aid him in the job. The angelic figure conferring with Santa in this charming portrait is reminiscent of one such character, the beloved Christkindl. Well-known in many parts of Europe, this sweet messenger is said to be sent from heaven to deliver presents at Christmastime.

A radiant figure, the winged Christkindl usually wears a flowing white robe and a sparkling crown — sometimes lighted with candles. Although genderless, this individual is often portrayed by a fair-haired young girl carrying the gift of a tree. At many German Christmas parties, she is the center of attention and distributes gifts to the children.

The name Christkindl (meaning Christ Child) originally referred to the Holy Infant, and in some European countries, He was believed to bring the gifts. The gifts were called "Christ bundles" and contained food, clothes, and small toys. Switches, or "Christ rods," were tied to a naughty child's bundle as a reminder to be good.

A Merry Christmas to you.

christmas aglow

Illuminated by the soft glow of Christmas candles, this kindly Santa makes another holiday delivery. The tiny dolls in his bag resemble Queen Victoria and her German husband, Prince Albert, who helped popularize the decorated Christmas tree in England in the early 1840's.

A German legend credits Martin Luther, a sixteenth century religious leader, with starting the custom of lighting the Christmas tree. According to the story, one cold December night, Luther looked up through the tree branches at the star-filled sky. He was so inspired by the awesome beauty that he hurried home and placed lighted candles on the branches of a tree. He used the candle-lit tree to illustrate the story of the Christ Child, whose birth had been heralded by a bright and shining star.

A merry CHRISTMAS

KRIS KRINGLE

he ray of light bathing this elfin figure brings to mind the religious origin of Kris Kringle, a forerunner of today's jolly Santa Claus. Similar to Santa in his giving nature, Kris Kringle takes his name from the Christkindl (meaning Christ Child), a gift-bearing character from northern Europe. Unlike our modern Santa, who places presents under the Christmas tree, Kris Kringle left gifts in the tree's branches.

When the Germans brought their beloved Christkindl to America, English-speaking children mispronounced the name so often that it became Krist Kingle or Kriss Kingle, and finally, by the 1860's, Kris Kringle.

As his name changed, so did his image. Soon, he became a very different character from his namesake, and his name was used interchangeably with that of Santa Claus.

Santa Claus Greetings!

man for all seasons

a s Santa travels around the globe, he's certain to encounter all kinds of weather. Yet it stretches the imagination for us to picture him trudging along beneath an umbrella.

This turn-of-the-century postcard is a good example of the freedom earlier artists had in the way they depicted Santa. Sometimes he was a tall, thin, stern-looking gentleman; at other times he was a round, twinkling-eyed little elf. Even an umbrella-toting Santa would not have seemed out of place back then. Later, as communication systems improved, a standard image of the gift-giver began to appear worldwide.

It was Dr. Clement Clarke Moore's poem, "The Night Before Christmas," that set the stage for the appearance of America's rosy-cheeked Santa. Illustrator Thomas Nast enhanced the picture when he dressed the chubby, elfin figure in the red suit we know today. Artist Haddon Sundblom added the final touches to Santa's contemporary look in his series of Coca-Cola® ads, which ran each year from 1931 until 1968.

A glad Christmas.

sweet dreams

Believing that Santa Claus won't come until they're asleep, children have always hurried to bed early the night before Christmas. Their dreams are filled with images of the wonderful treasures they hope to find when they awaken, whether it's visions of sugarplums, darling baby dolls, or bright red wagons.

Here, as Father Christmas takes a few seconds to peek in on a sweet Christmas dreamer, his smile conveys his joy at having made her dreams come true.

A HAPPY CHRISTMAS.

all-american santa

D ressed in patriotic colors, Santa Claus marches through the snow to spread the Christmas spirit. The toy drum, bugle, sabres, and tiny American flag reflect the tremendous effect the Civil War had on America — even touching its cherished image of Santa Claus.

During this tense period, the Christmas celebration was one of the few distractions from the battlefield. However, as shown here in Santa's grave expression, the joy of the season was tainted by the grim consequences of war. Children in the South worried that Santa wouldn't be able to cross Union blockades, and both sides used the benevolent figure as a propaganda tool.

During the war, Thomas Nast (who would later illustrate the holiday poem, "The Night Before Christmas") was a political cartoonist for *Harper's Weekly* magazine. The cover of the 1864 Christmas issue featured his drawing of the gift-giver dressed in a star-spangled jacket and striped pants delivering presents to Northern soldiers.

President Abraham Lincoln even employed Nast to create an American image for the holiday figure and remarked that with his Santa Claus drawings, Nast had become the North's best recruiting agent.

merry olde gent

Shown on page 6.

Merry Olde Gent was stitched over 2 fabric threads on a 16" x 19" piece of Cream Lugana (25 ct). Three strands of floss were used for Cross Stitch, 2 for gold metallic Backstitch, and 1 for all other Backstitch.

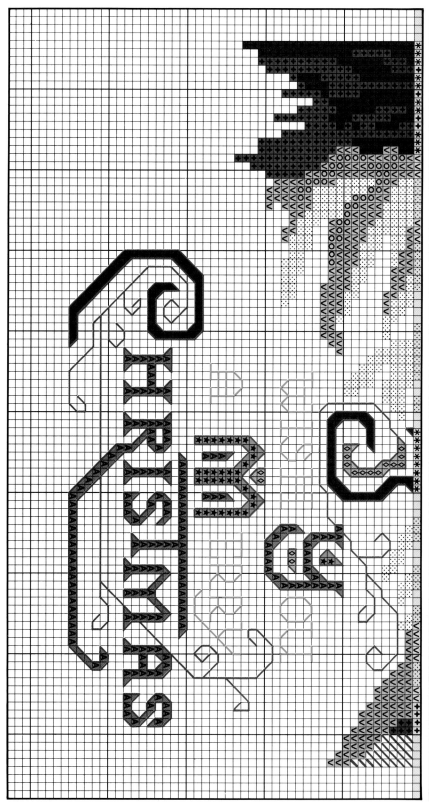

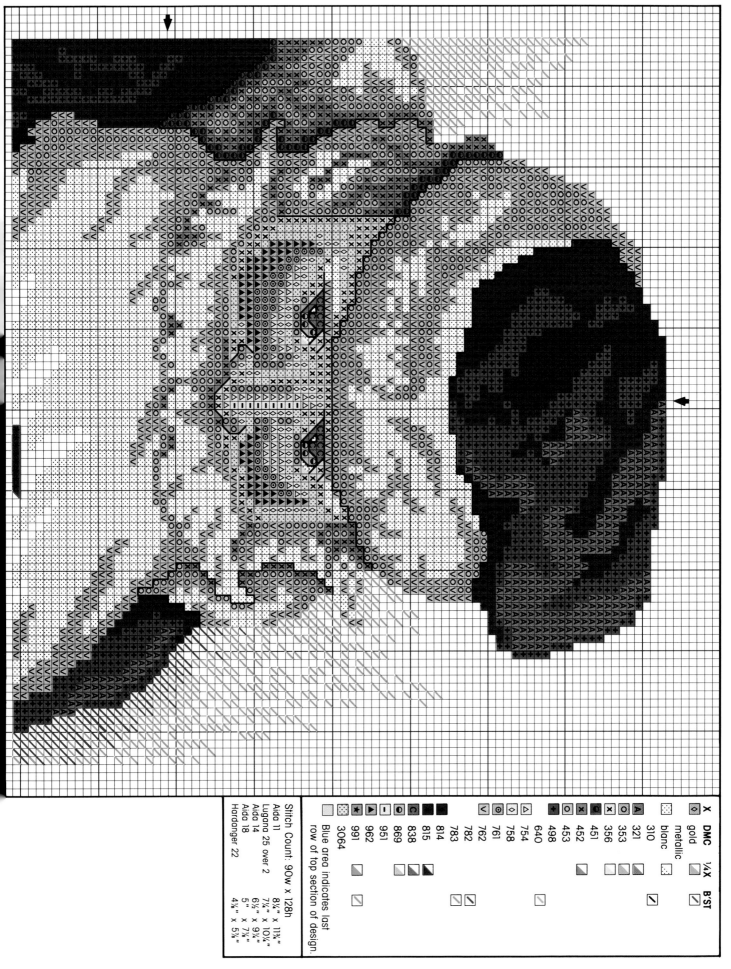

O, STARRY NIGHT

Shown on page 8.

O, Starry Night was stitched over 2 fabric threads on a 15" x 19" piece of Delicate Teal Jobelan (28 ct). Two strands of floss were used for Cross Stitch, 1 for Half Cross Stitch, 1 for Backstitch, and 1 for French Knots.

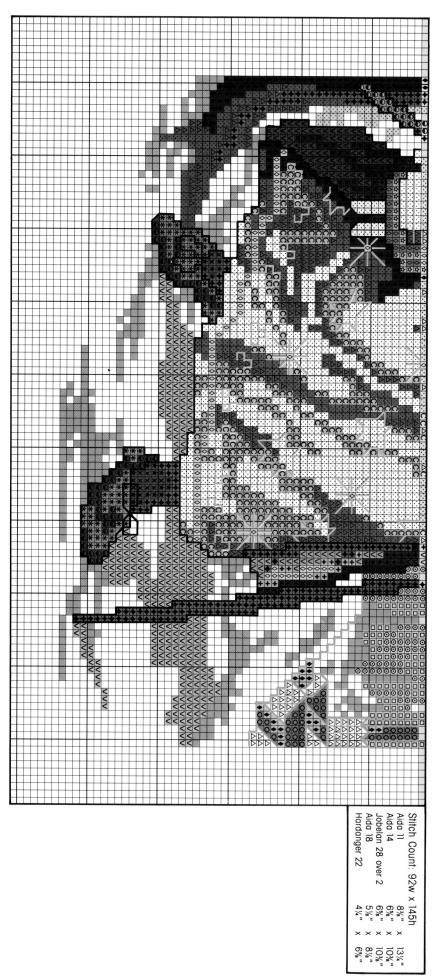

Stitch Count: 92w x 145h

Aida 11	8⅜" x 13¼"
Aida 14	6⅝" x 10⅜"
Jobelan 28 over 2	6⅝" x 10⅜"
Aida 18	5⅛" x 8⅛"
Hardanger 22	4¼" x 6⅝"

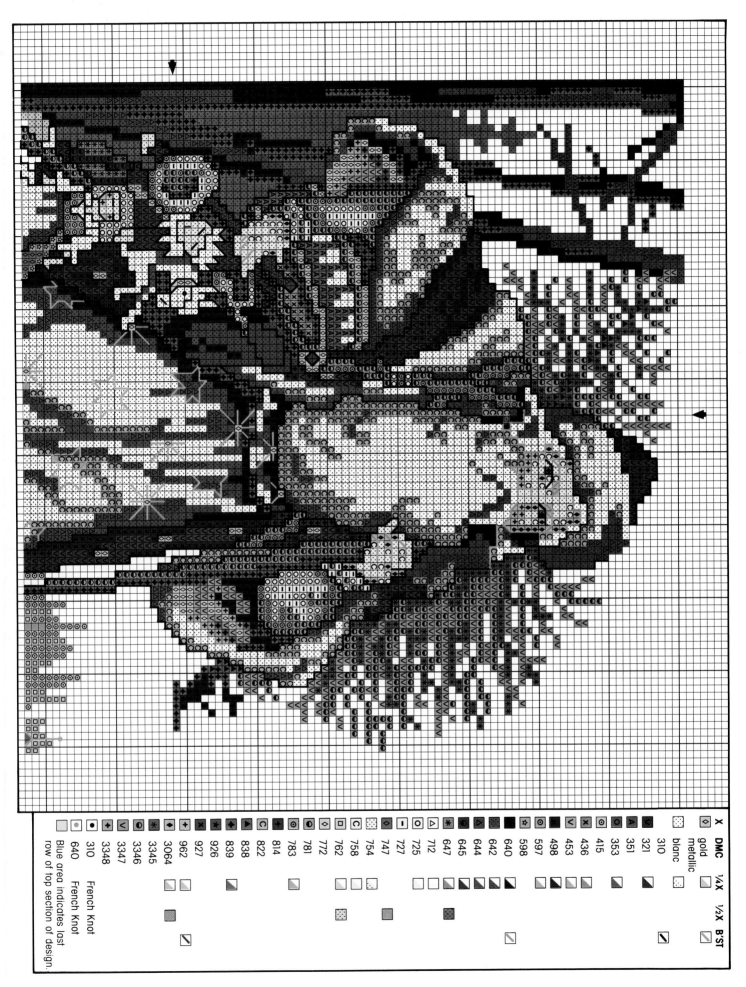

making a list

Shown on page 10.

Making A List was stitched over 2 fabric threads on a 15" x 18" piece of Moss Green Lugana (25 ct). Three strands of floss were used for Cross Stitch and 1 for Backstitch.

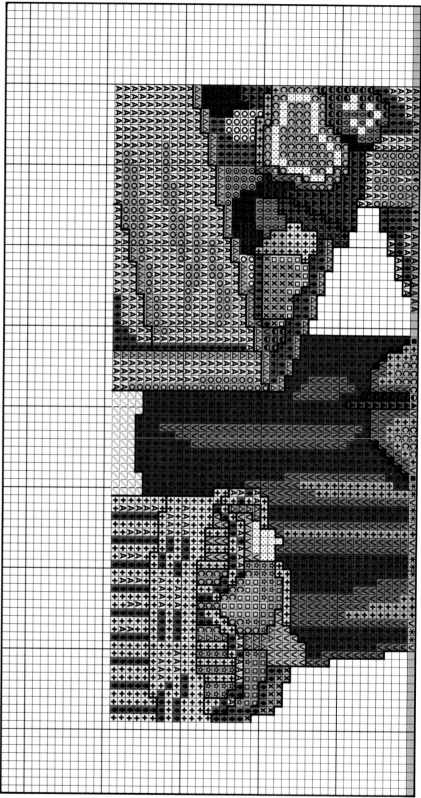

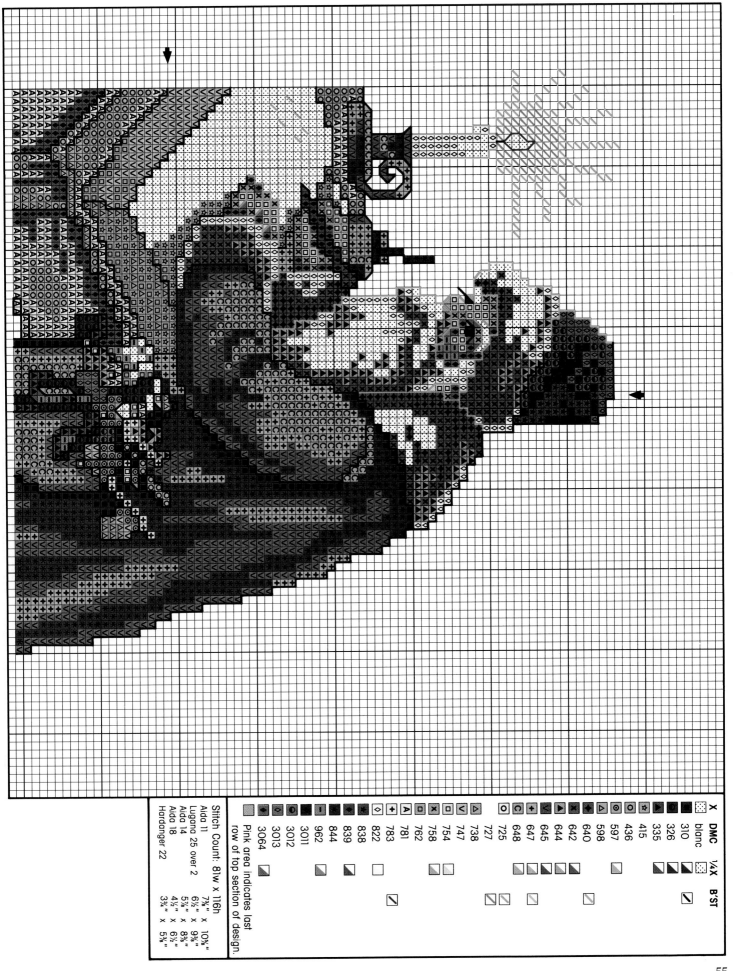

weihnachtsmann

Shown on page 12.

Weihnachtsmann was stitched over 2 fabric threads on a 14" x 18" piece of Raw Belfast Linen (32 ct). Two strands of floss were used for Cross Stitch, 1 for Half Cross Stitch, 1 for Backstitch, and 1 for French Knots.

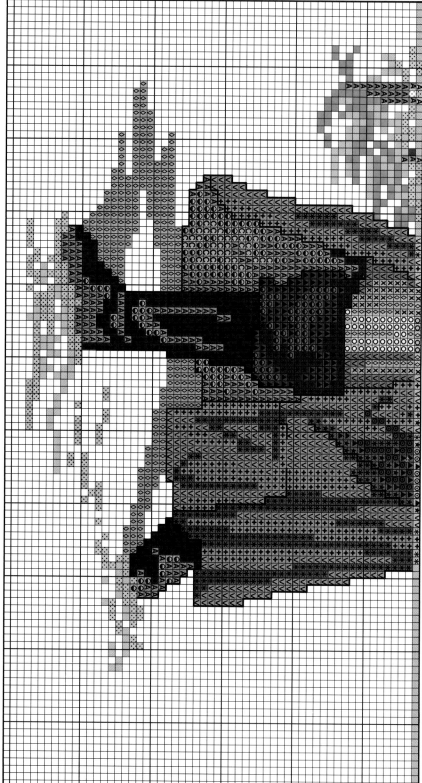

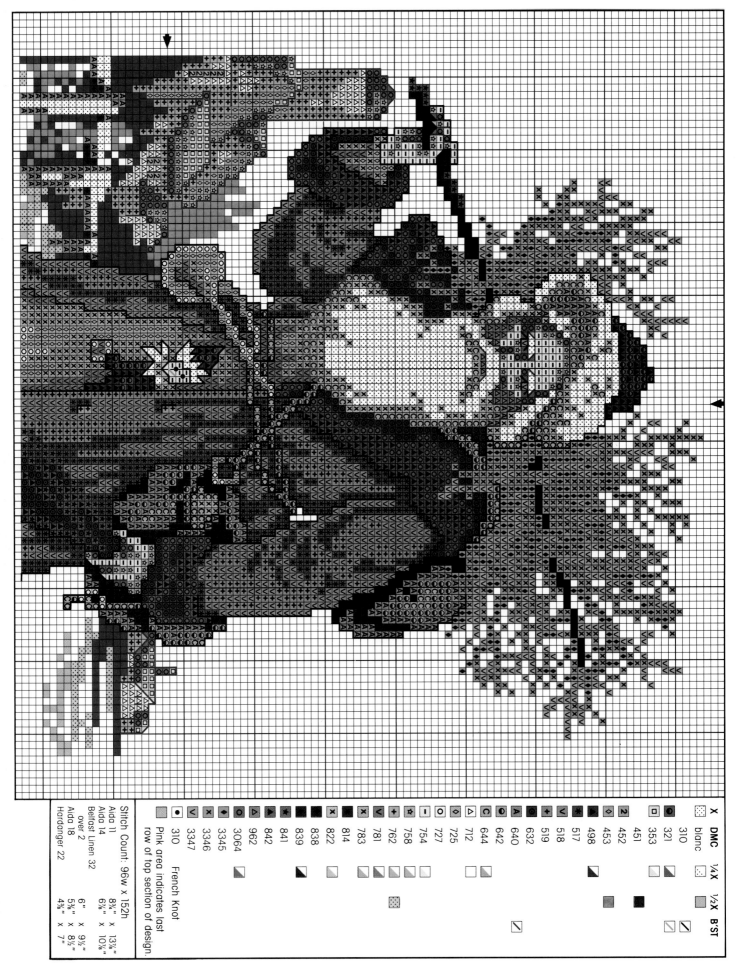

X	DMC	¼X	½X	B'ST
	blanc			
	310			
	321			
	353			
	451			
	452			
	453			
	498			
	517			
	518			
	519			
	632			
	640			
	642			
	644			
	712			
	725			
	727			
	754			
	758			
	762			
	781			
	783			
	814			
	822			
	838			
	839			
	841			
	842			
	962			
	3064			
	3345			
	3346			
	3347			

310 French Knot

Pink area indicates last row of top section of design.

Stitch Count: 96w x 152h
Aida 11   8¾" x 13⅞"
Aida 14   6⅞" x 10⅞"
Belfast Linen 32
  over 2   6" x 9½"
Aida 18   5⅜" x 8½"
Hardanger 22   4⅜" x 7"

gentle st. nick

Shown on page 14.

Gentle St. Nick was stitched over 2 fabric threads on a 14" x 17" piece of Raw Belfast Linen (32 ct). Two strands of floss were used for Cross Stitch, 1 for Backstitch, and 1 for French Knots.

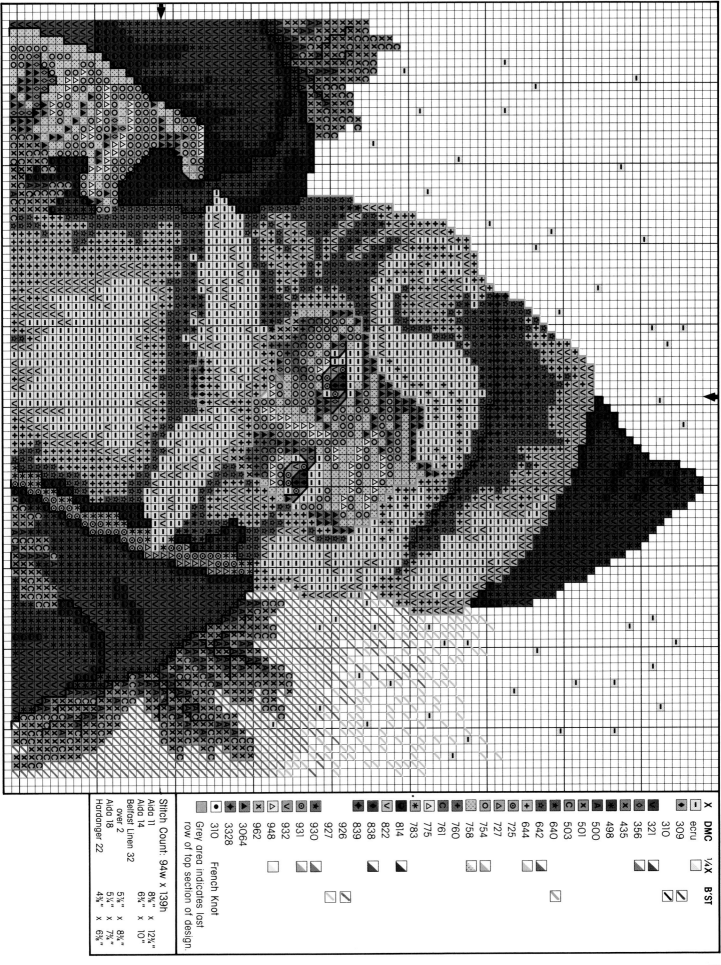

Memorable Stroll

Shown on page 16.

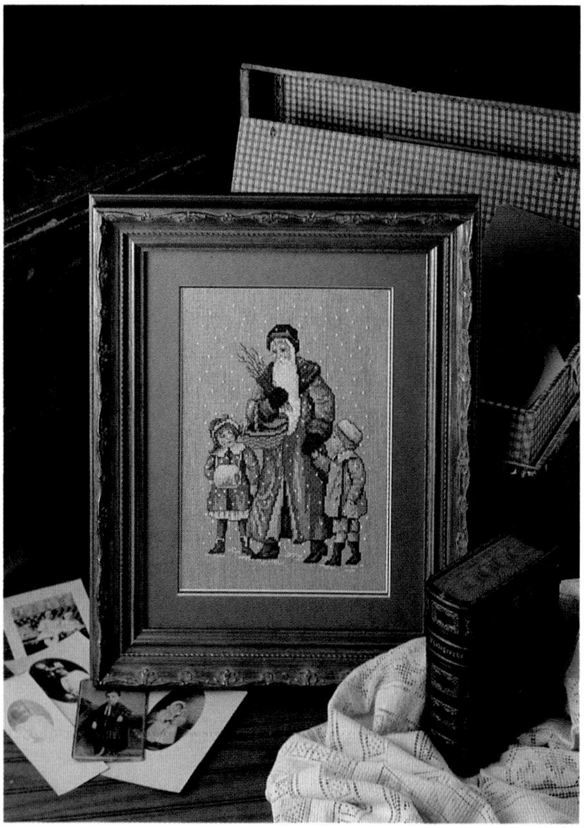

Memorable Stroll was stitched over 2 fabric threads on a 14" x 17" piece of Raw Belfast Linen (32 ct). Two strands of floss were used for Cross Stitch and 1 for Backstitch.

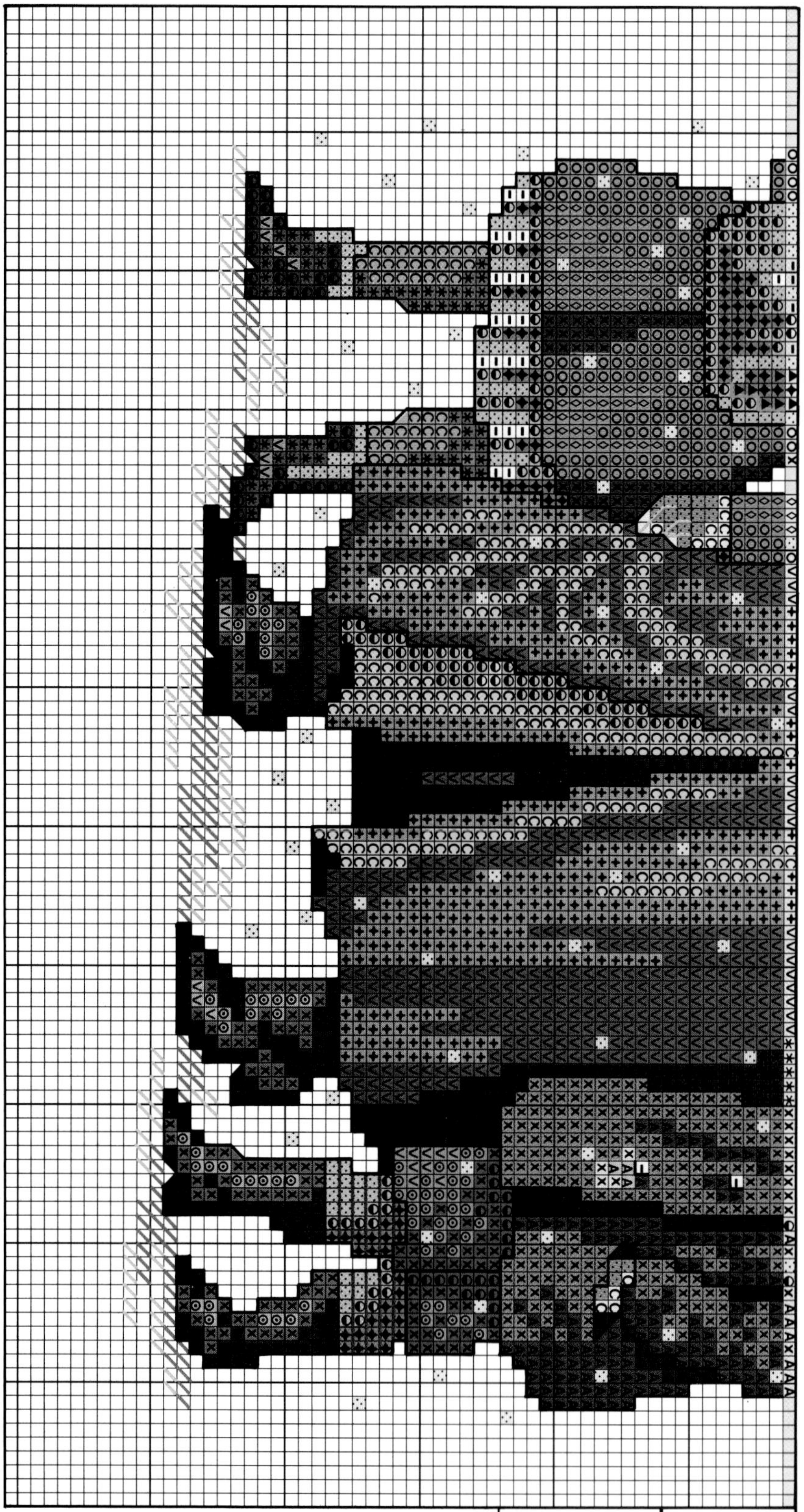

+ 3347
C 3348
Blue area indicates last row of top section of design.

Stitch Count: 98w x 140h

Aida 11	9"	x	12¾"
Aida 14	7"	x	10"
Belfast Linen 32 over 2	6⅛"	x	8¾"
Aida 18	5½"	x	7⅞"
Hardanger 22	4½"	x	6⅜"

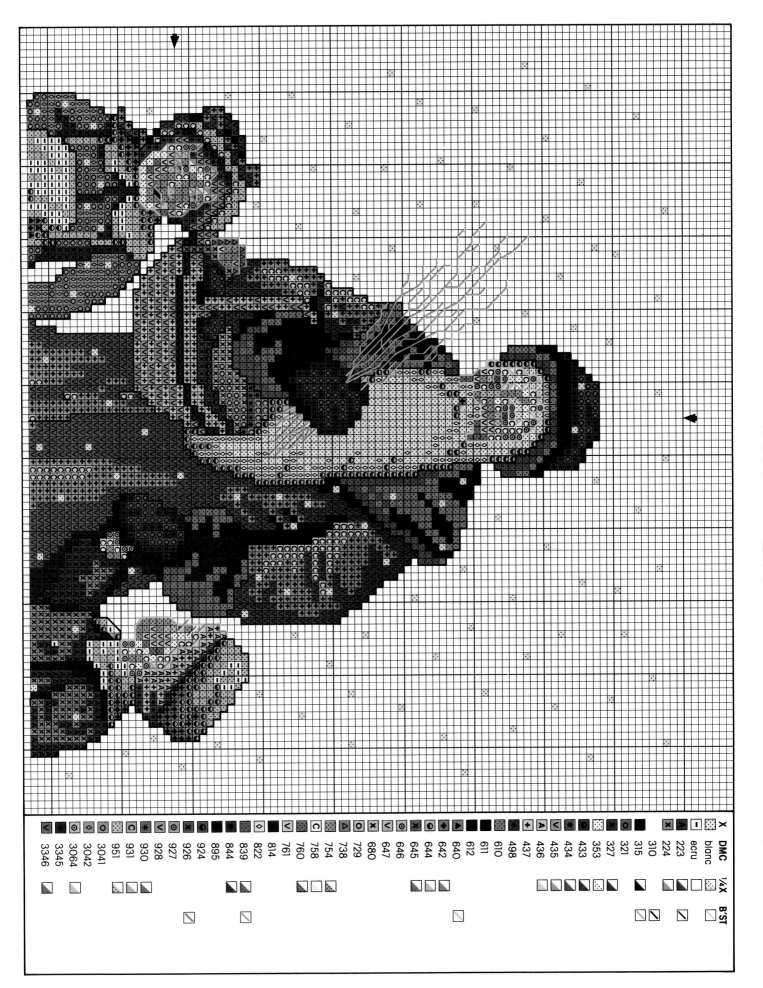

chRistmas RideR

Shown on page 18.

Christmas Rider was stitched over 2 fabric threads on a 16" x 19" piece of Clay Linda (27 ct). Two strands of floss were used for Cross Stitch, 1 for Backstitch, and 1 for French Knot.

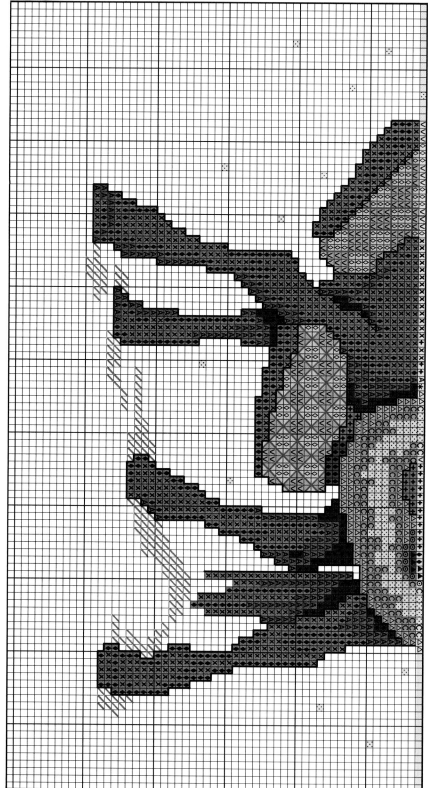

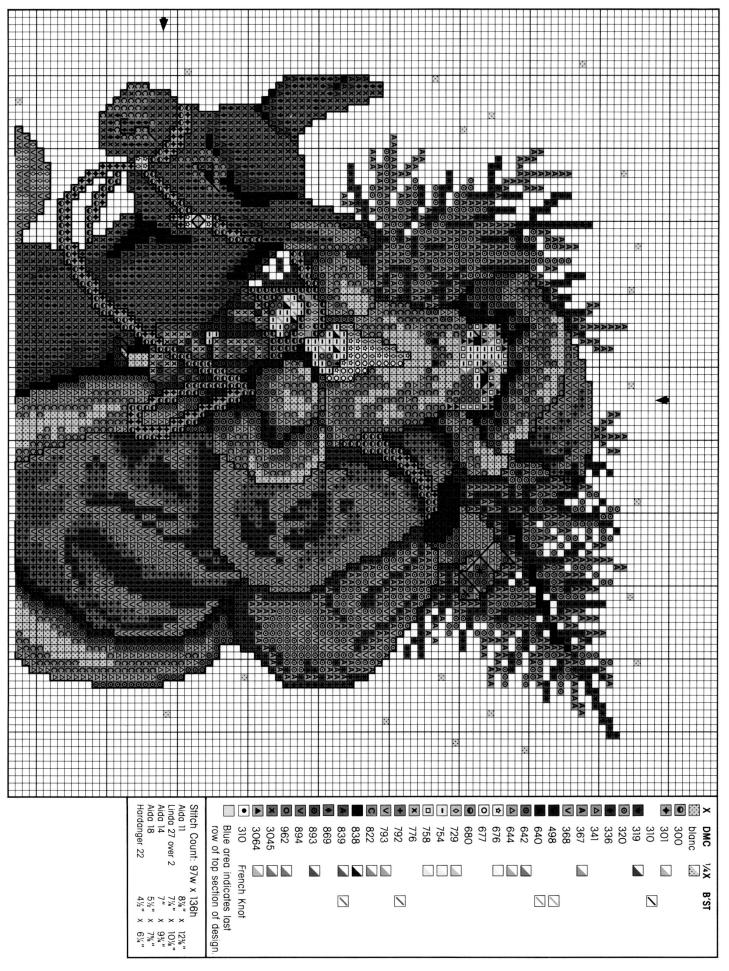

X	DMC	¼X	B'ST
	blanc		
	300		
	301		
	310		
	319		
	320		
	336		
	341		
	367		
	368		
	498		
	642		
	644		
	676		
	677		
	680		
	729		
	754		
	758		
	776		
	792		
	793		
	822		
	838		
	839		
	869		
	893		
	894		
	962		
	3045		
	3064		
	310	French Knot	

Blue area indicates last
row of top section of design.

Stitch Count: 97w x 136h
Aida 11   8¾" x 12⅜"
Aida 14   7" x 9¾"
Aida 18   5½" x 7⅝"
Hardanger 22   4½" x 6¼"
Linda 27 over 2 7¼" x 10⅛"

traveling companions

Shown on page 20.

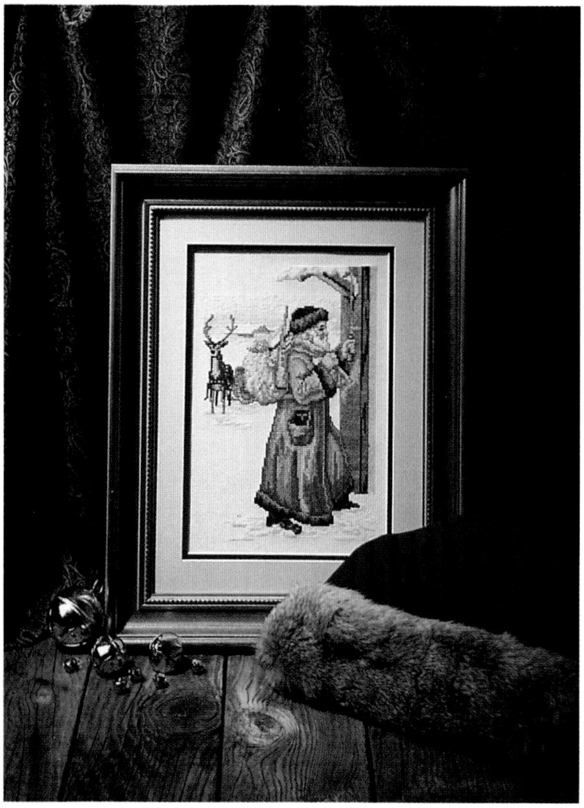

Traveling Companions was stitched over 2 fabric threads on a 16" x 20" piece of Cream Lugana (25 ct). Three strands of floss were used for Cross Stitch, 1 for Half Cross Stitch, 1 for Backstitch, and 1 for French Knots.

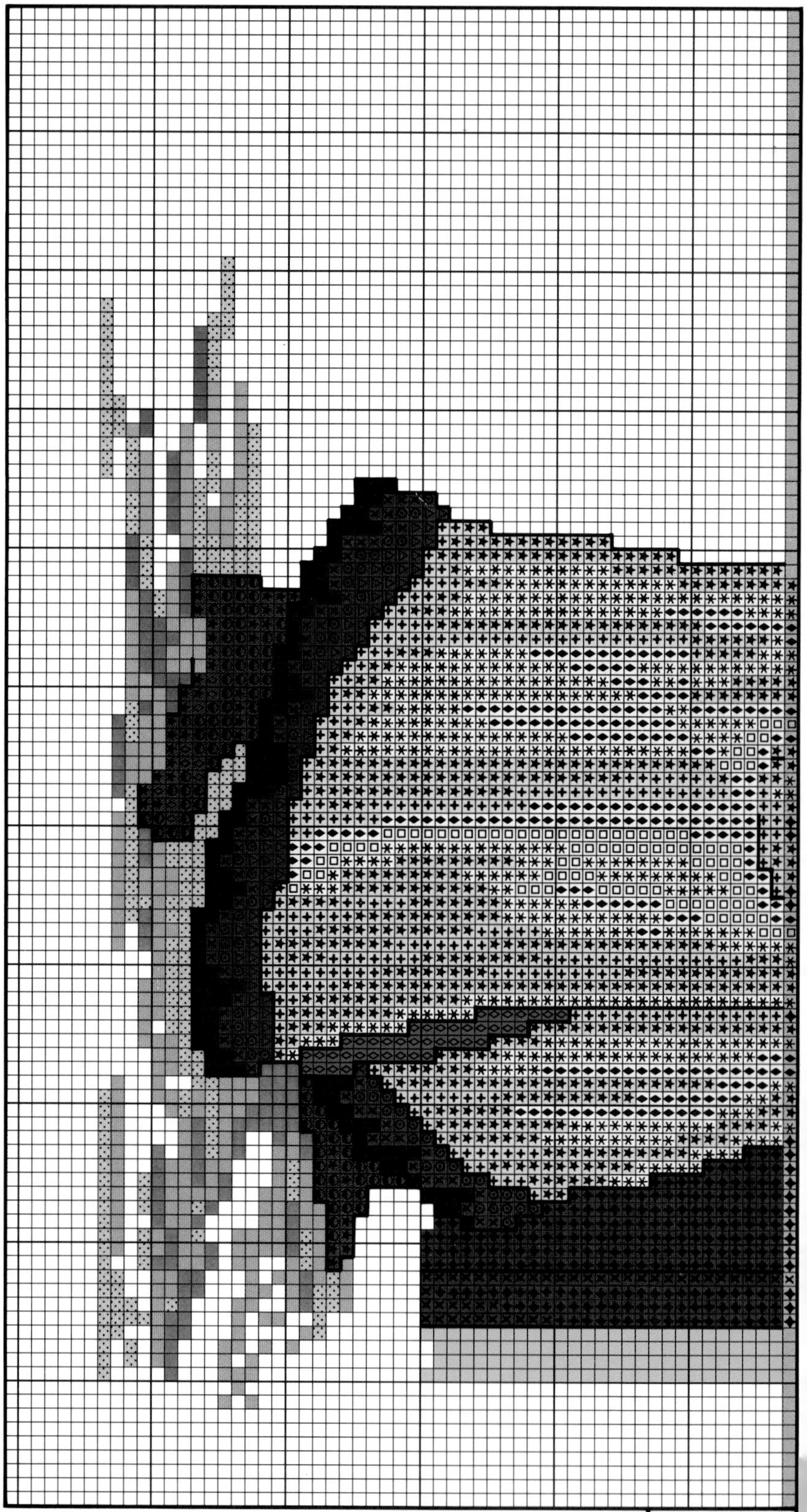

Stitch Count: 95w x 144h

Aida 11	8¾" x 13⅛"
Lugana 25 over 2	7⅝" x 11⅝"
Aida 14	6⅞" x 10⅜"
Aida 18	5⅜" x 8"
Hardanger 22	4⅜" x 6⅝"

father christmas

Shown on page 22.

Father Christmas was stitched over 2 fabric threads on a 15" x 16" piece of Cream Lugana (25 ct). Three strands of floss were used for Cross Stitch and 1 for Backstitch.

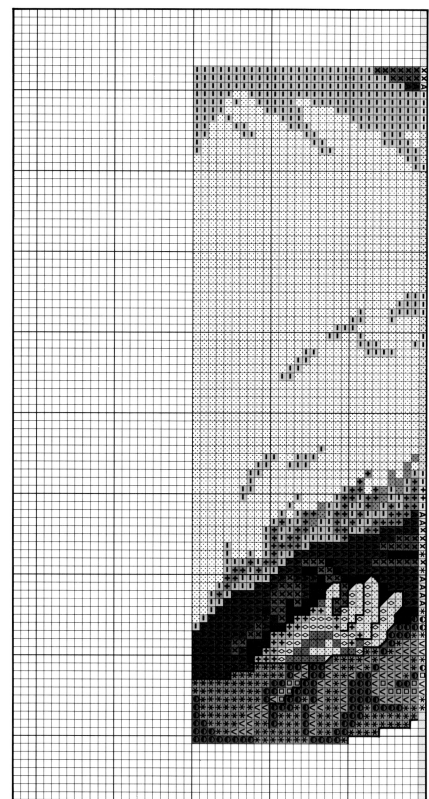

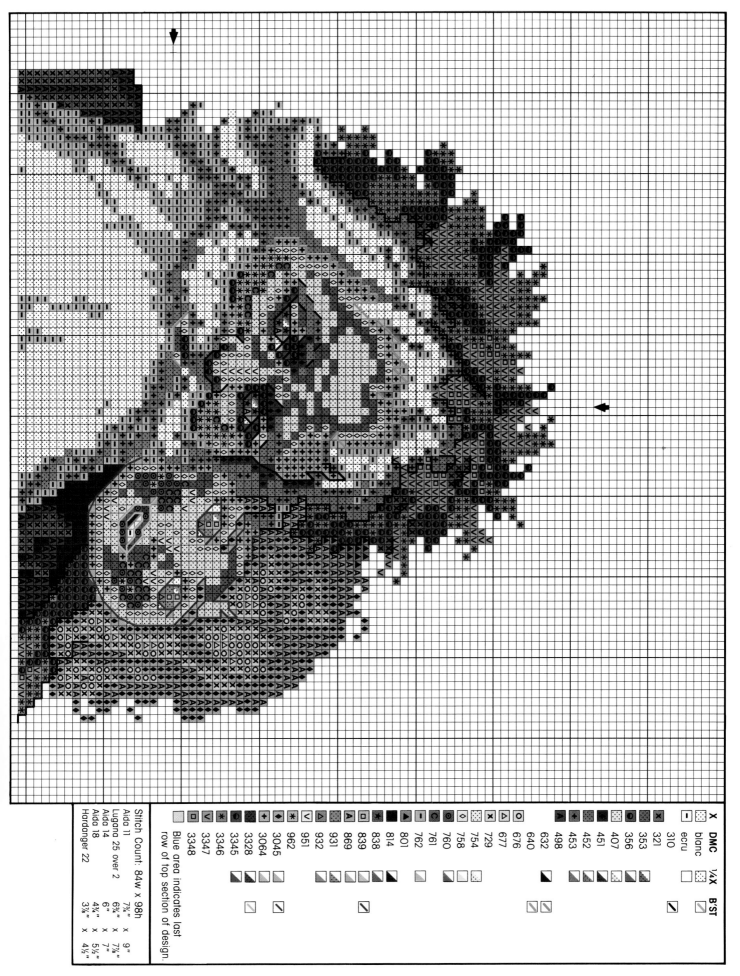

EVER GREEN, EVER GIVING

Shown on page 24.

Ever Green, Ever Giving was stitched over 2 fabric threads on a 16" x 19" piece of Tile Blue Linda (27 ct). Three strands of floss were used for Cross Stitch, 1 for Backstitch, and 1 for French Knots.

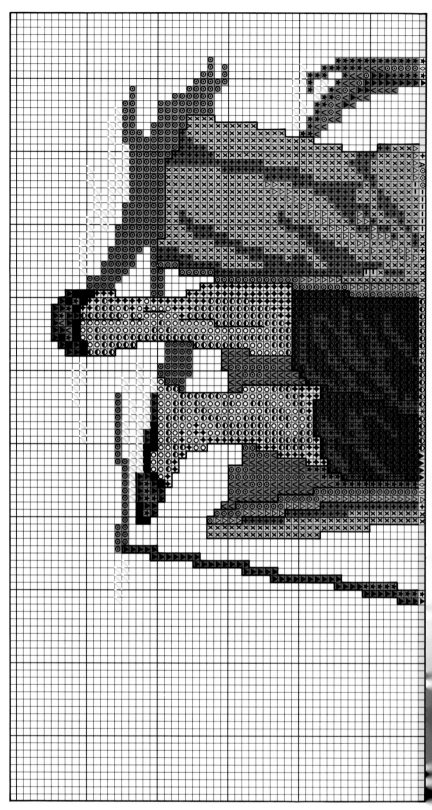

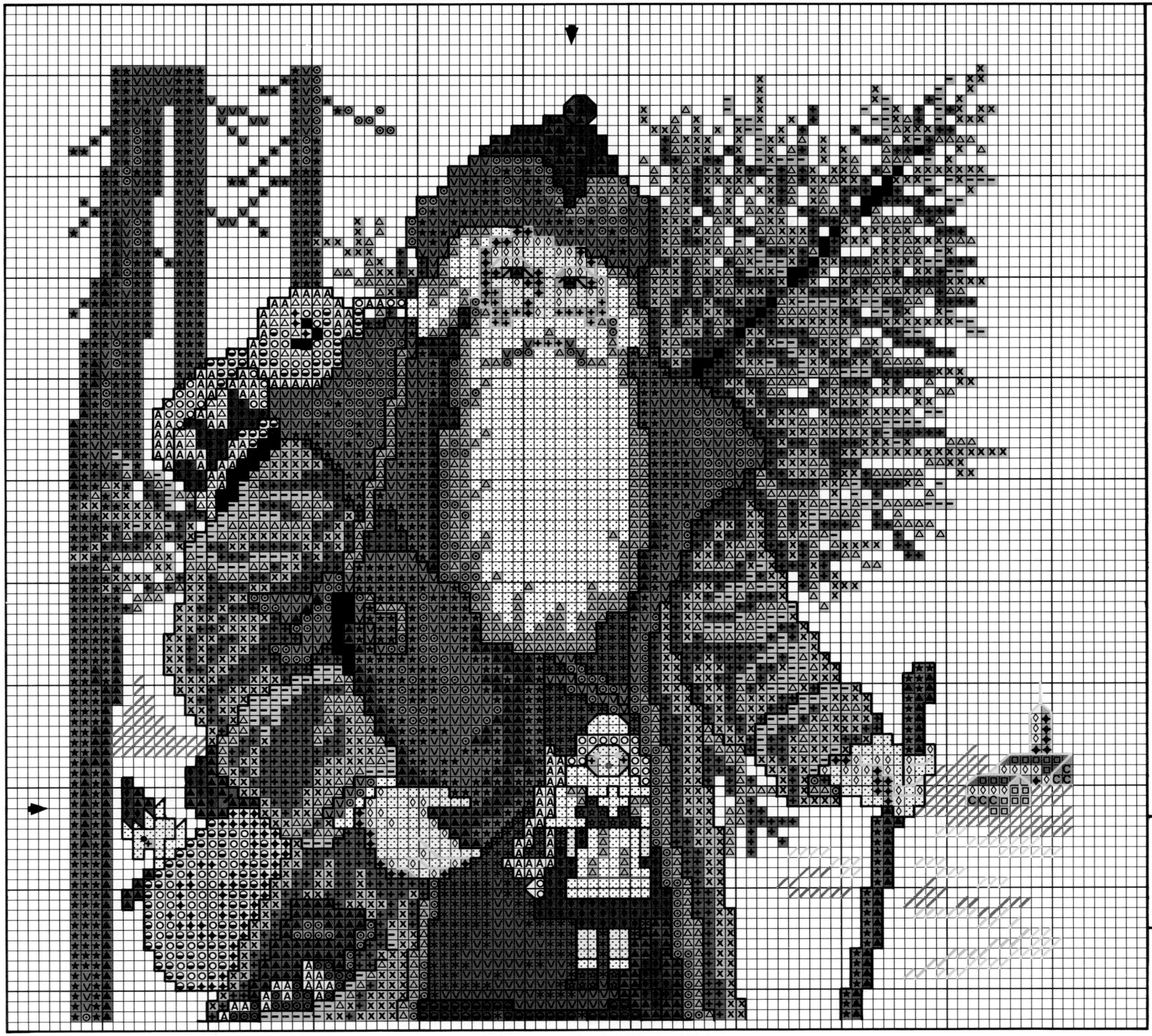

DMC	¼X	B'ST
blanc	■	■
310		■
315	■	
321	■	■
351		
353	■	
452		■
453		■
498	■	
640		■
642		
644		
712	■	
725		
726		
754	■	
758	■	
762	■	■
780		
781		
783	■	
814		
822		
838		
839		
902		
962	■	
3041		
3064	■	■
3345		
3346		
3347		
3348		
310 French Knot		
839 French Knot		
962 French Knot		

Blue area indicates last row of top section of design.

Stitch Count: 95w x 146h

Aida 11	8¾"	x	13⅜"
Linda 27 over 2	7⅛"	x	10⅞"
Aida 14	6⅞"	x	10½"
Aida 18	5⅜"	x	8⅛"
Hardanger 22	4⅜"	x	6¾"

patron saint of children

Shown on page 26.

Patron Saint of Children was stitched over 2 fabric threads on a 16" x 19" piece of Dirty Linen Linda (27 ct). Two strands of floss were used for Cross Stitch, 3 for gold metallic Cross Stitch, 2 for gold metallic Backstitch, and 1 for all other Backstitch.

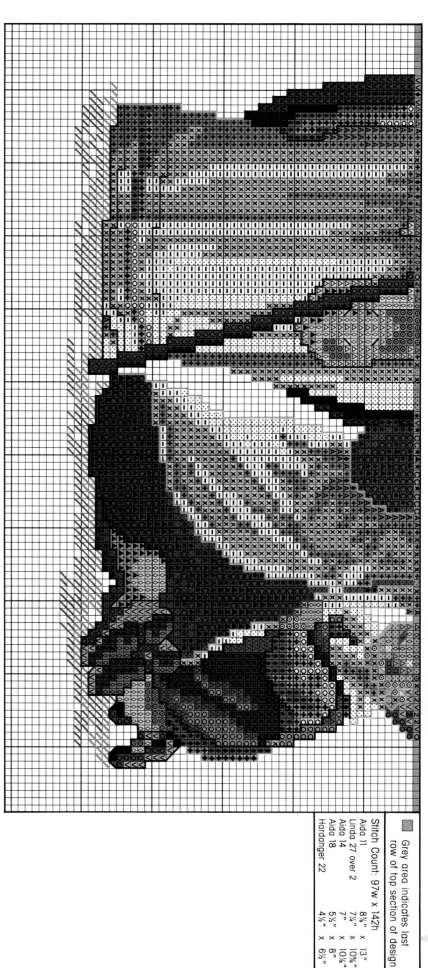

Grey area indicates last row of top section of design

Stitch Count:	97w x	142h
Aida 11	8⅞" x	13"
Aida 11	7¼" x	10⅝"
Linda 27 over 2	7" x	10⅛"
Aida 14	5½" x	8"
Aida 18	4½" x	6½"
Hardanger 22		

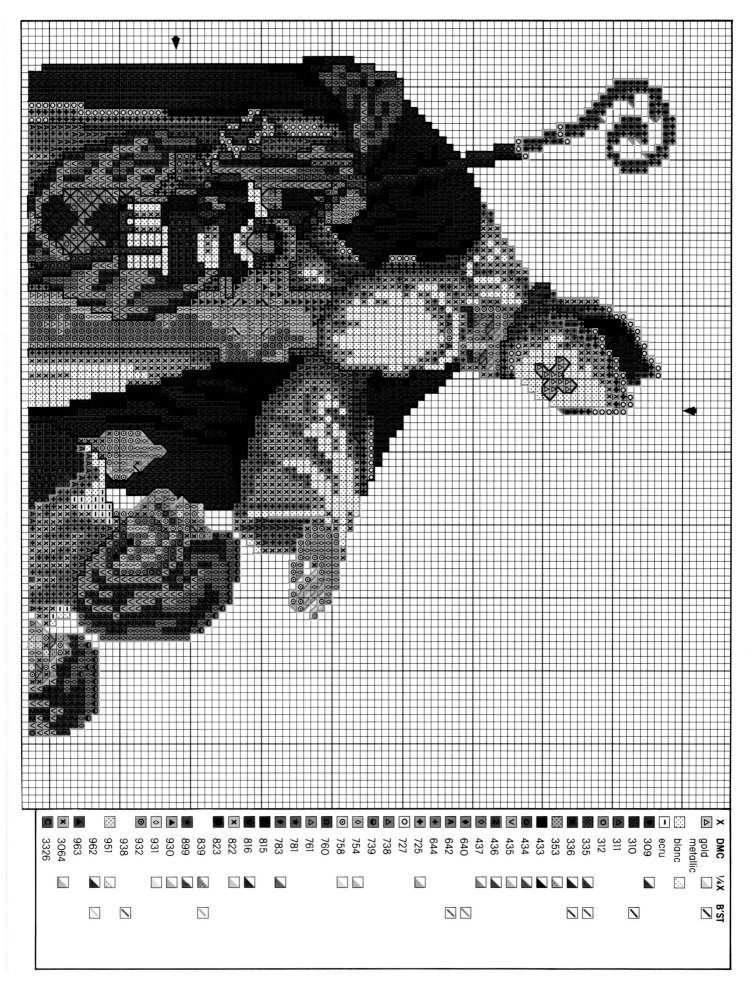

RINGING IN christmas

Shown on page 28.

Ringing In Christmas was stitched over 2 fabric threads on a 15" x 19" piece of Cream Lugana (25 ct). Three strands of floss were used for Cross Stitch, 1 for Half Cross Stitch, 1 for Backstitch, and 1 for French Knots.

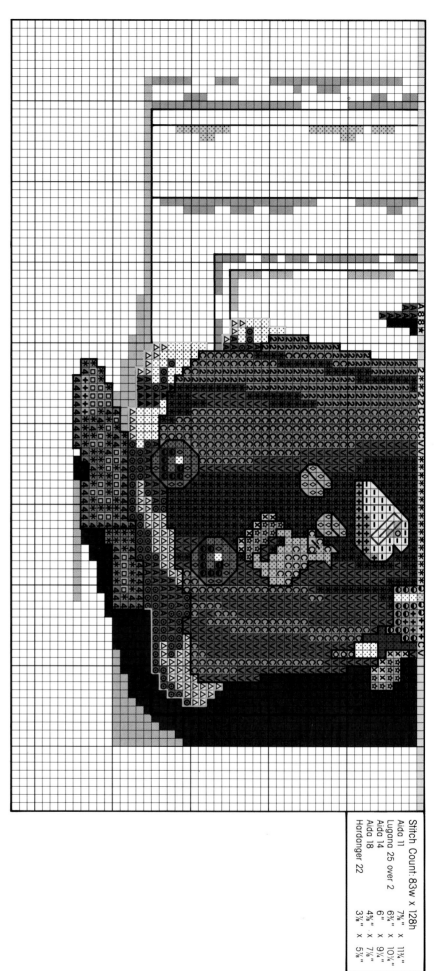

Stitch Count: 83w x 128h
Aida 11   7⅝" x 11¾"
Lugana 25 over 2 6⅝" x 10¼"
Aida 14   6"   x 9¼"
Aida 18   4⅝" x 7⅛"
Hardanger 22   3⅞" x 5⅝"

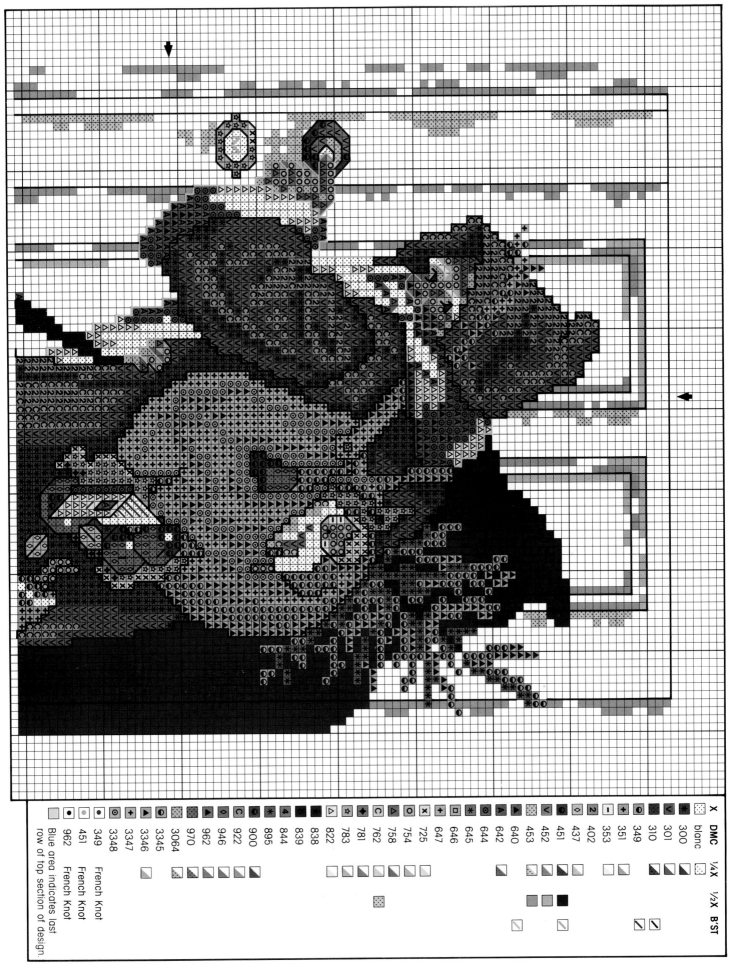

X	DMC	¼X	½X	B'ST
⬚	blanc	⬚		
⊡	300			
●	301			
⬛	310			
◧	353			
◧	351	◧		⬊
◨	349	◨		⬊
⬛	310	⬛		
⬚	402	⬚		
2	437			
I	451	◧		
+	452	◧		⬊
◑	453	◧		
⬛	640	⬛		⬊
◤	642	◤		
▶	644			
◫	645			
⬚	646			
⊡	647			
✳	725			
O	754	◧	⬚	
✕	758	◧		
+	762	◧		
▣	781	◧		
✳	783	◧		
◫	822	◧	◧	
▷	838			
⬟	839			
◆	844			
◪	895			
C	900	◪		
◑	922	◪		
O	946	◪		
✕	962	◪		
+	970	◪		
◩	3064	◩	⊡	
✳	3345			
◫	3346			
▲	3347			
◕	3348			

449 French Knot
451 French Knot
962 French Knot

Blue area indicates last
row of top section of design.

73

BRINGING CHRISTMAS SPIRIT

Shown on page 30.

Bringing Christmas Spirit was stitched over 2 fabric threads on a 15" x 18" piece of Ivory Lugana (25 ct). Three strands of floss were used for Cross Stitch, 1 for Backstitch, and 1 for French Knots.

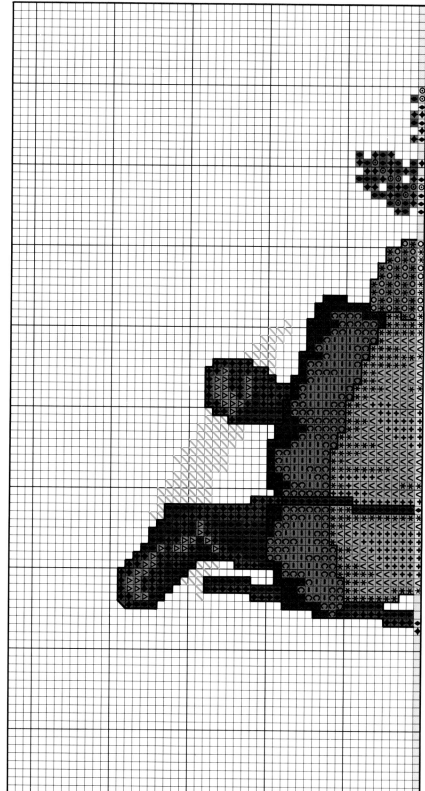

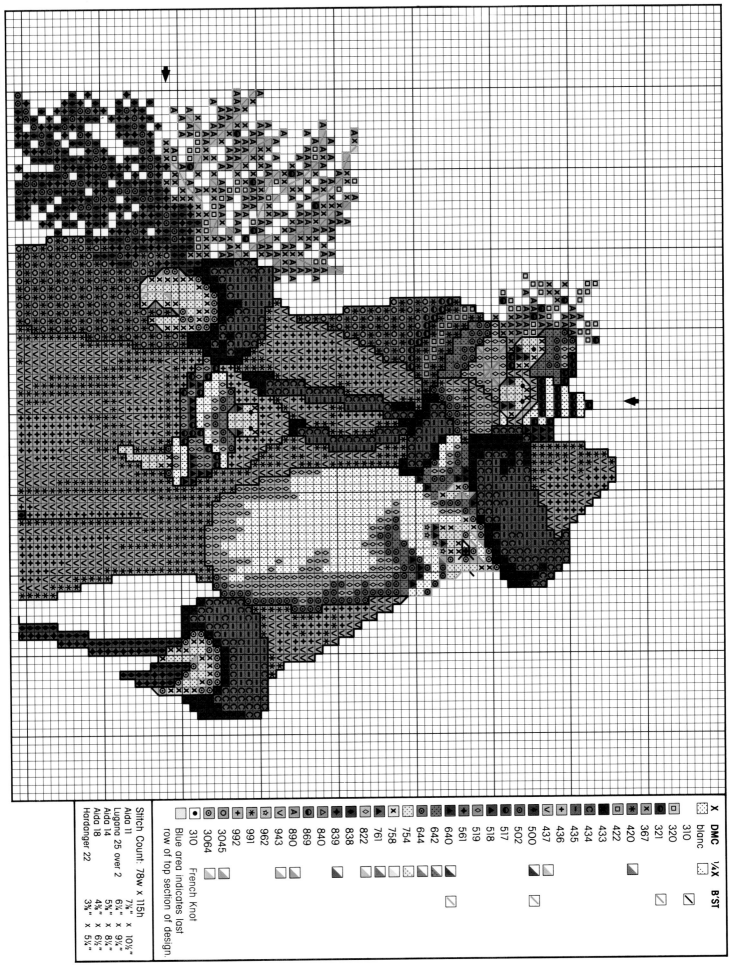

GRANDFATHERLY GENT

Shown on page 32.

Grandfatherly Gent was stitched over 2 fabric threads on a 15" x 18" piece of Cream Lugana (25 ct). Three strands of floss were used for Cross Stitch and 1 for Backstitch.

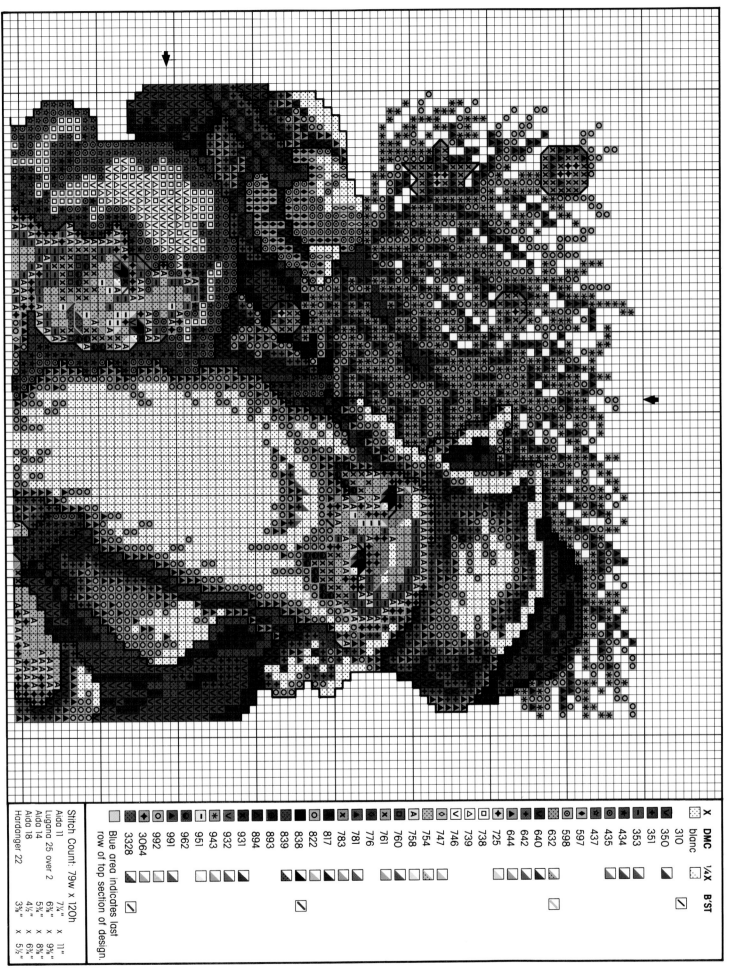

a splendid sight

Shown on page 34.

A Splendid Sight was stitched over 2 fabric threads on a 16" x 19" piece of Misty Grey Linen (26 ct). Two strands of floss were used for Cross Stitch and 1 for Backstitch.

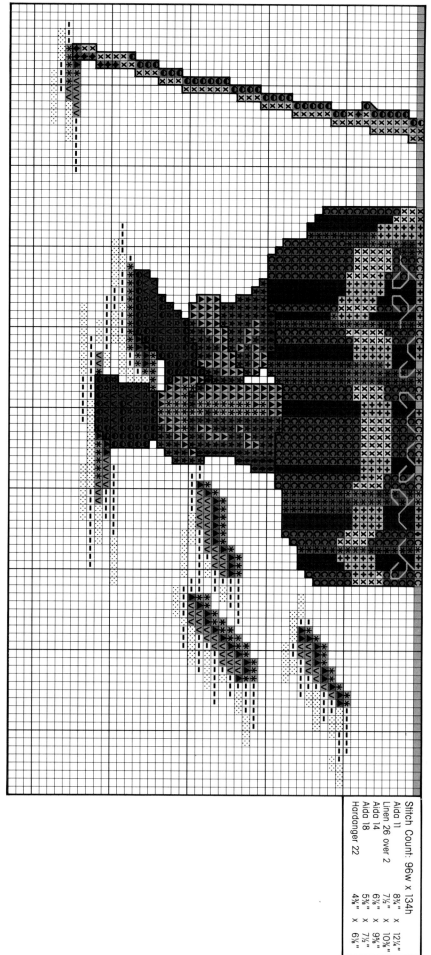

Stitch Count: 96w x 134h		
Aida 11	8¾"	x 12¼"
Linen 26 over 2	7½"	x 10⅜"
Aida 14	6⅞"	x 9⅝"
Aida 18	5⅜"	x 7½"
Hardanger 22	4⅜"	x 6⅛"

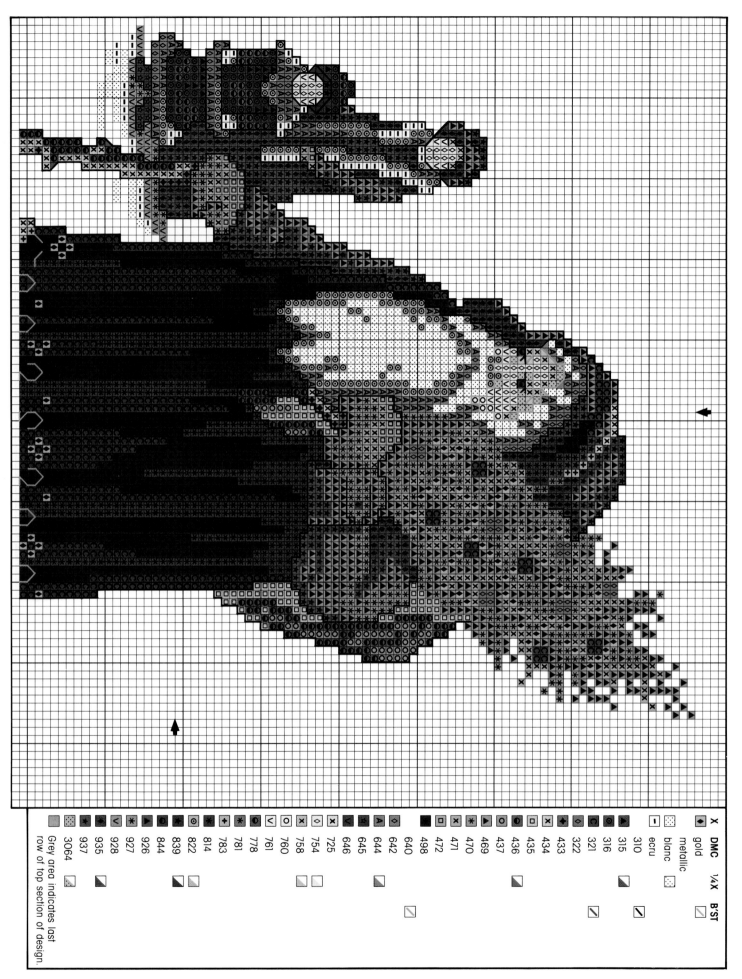

miles to go

Shown on page 36.

Miles to Go was stitched over 2 fabric threads on a 16" x 19" piece of Black Lugana (25 ct). Four strands of floss were used for Cross Stitch, 1 for Backstitch, and 1 for French Knots.

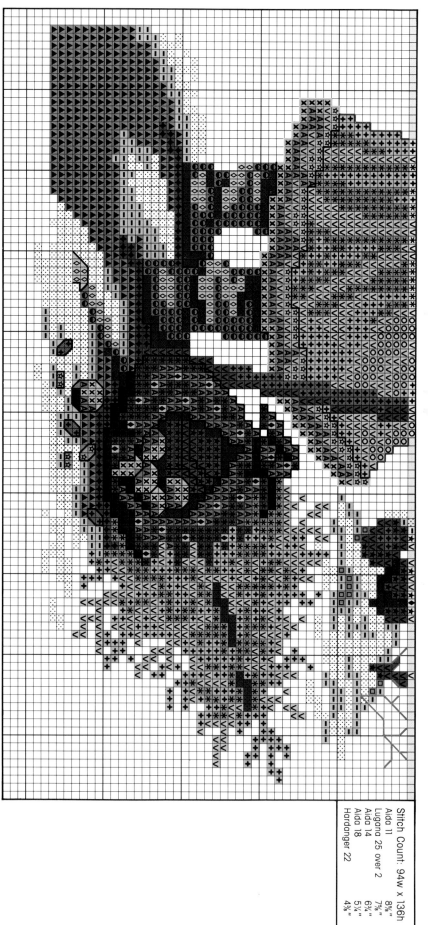

Stitch Count: 94w x 136h	
Aida 11	8⅝" × 12⅜"
Lugana 25 over 2	7⅝" × 11"
Aida 14	6¾" × 9¾"
Aida 18	5¼" × 7⅝"
Hardanger 22	4⅜" × 6¼"

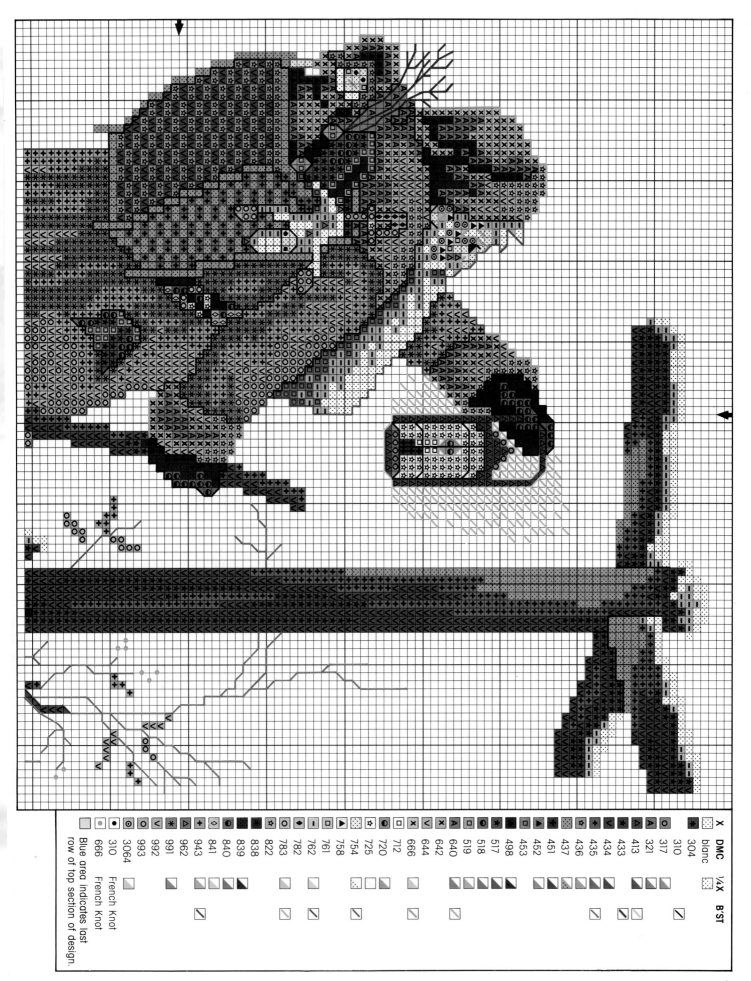

santa's helper

Shown on page 38.

Santa's Helper was stitched over 2 fabric threads on a 16" x 19" piece of Cream Lugana (25 ct). Three strands of floss were used for Cross Stitch, 1 for Backstitch, and 1 for French Knots.

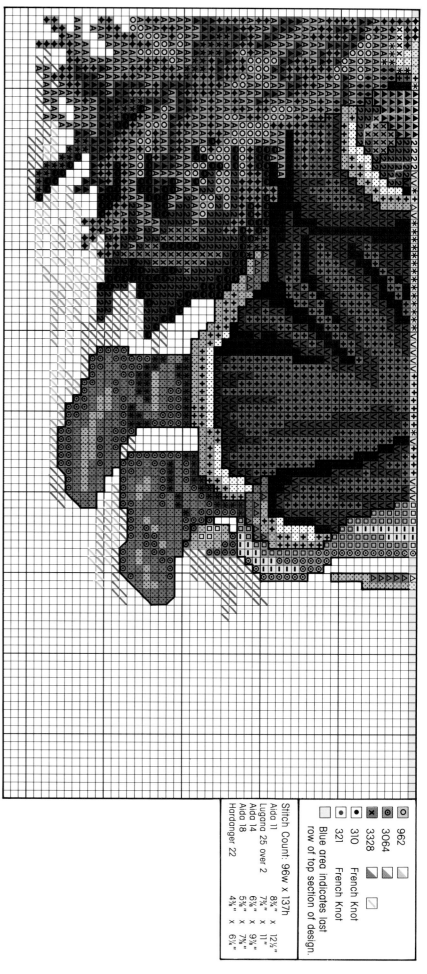

			962
			3064
			3328
			310 French Knot
			321 French Knot

Blue area indicates last row of top section of design.

Stitch Count: 96w x 137h

Aida 11	8¾" x 12½"
Aida 14	7¾" x 11"
Lugana 25 over 2	6⅞" x 9⅞"
Aida 18	5⅜" x 7⅝"
Hardanger 22	4⅜" x 6¼"

82

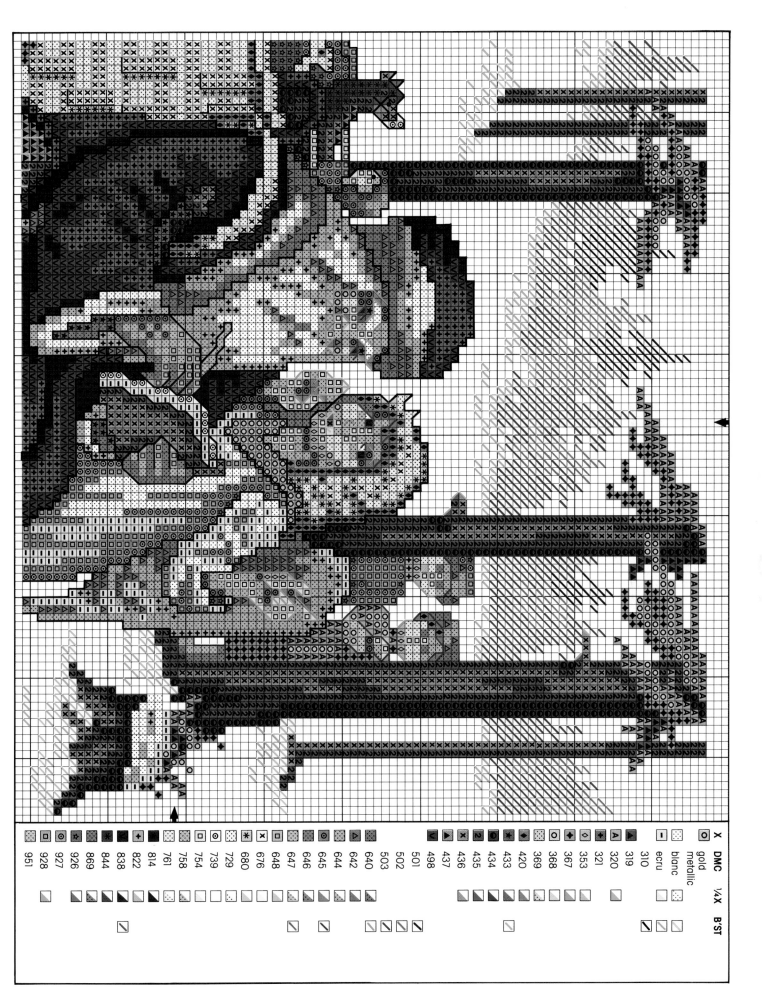

X	DMC	¼X	B'ST
▨	gold		
⊙	metallic		
	blanc		
	ecru		
▌	951	◨	
▨	928	◨	
▨	927	◨	◺
▨	926	◨	
▨	869	◨	
▨	844	◨	
▨	838	◨	
▨	822	◨	
▨	814	◨	
▨	761	◨	
▨	758	◨	
▨	754	◨	
▨	739	◨	◺
▨	729	◨	
▨	680	◨	◺
▨	676	◨	
▨	648	◨	◺
▨	647	◨	◺ ◺
▨	646	◨	
▨	645	◨	◺
▨	644	◨	
▨	642	◨	
▨	640	◨	
▨	503	◨	◺
▨	502	◨	
▨	501	◨	
▨	498	◨	
▨	437	◨	
▨	436	◨	
▨	435	◨	
▨	434	◨	
▨	433	◨	
▨	420	◨	
▨	369	◨	
▨	368	◨	
▨	367	◨	
▨	353	◨	
▨	321	◨	
▨	320	◨	◺
▨	319	◨	◺ ◺
▨	310	◨	

83

Christmas Aglow

Shown on page 40.

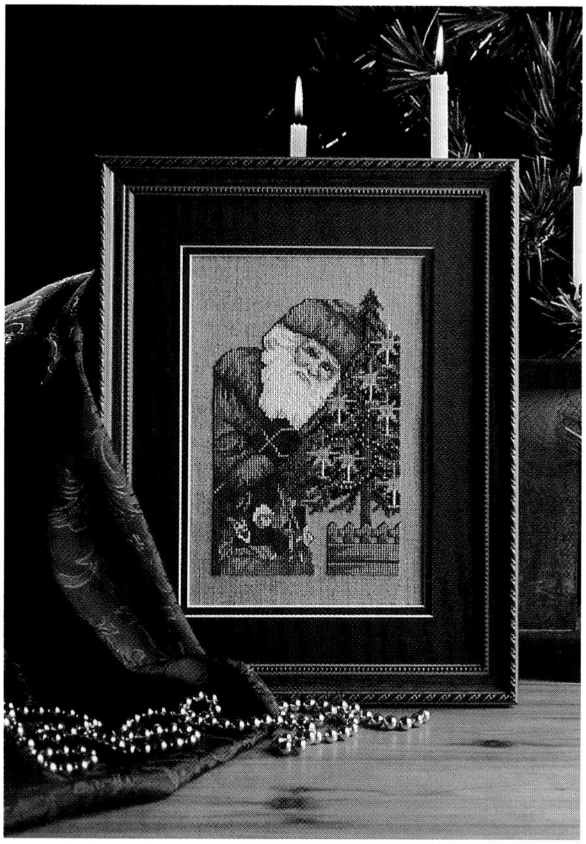

Christmas Aglow was stitched over 2 fabric threads on a 13" x 16" piece of Raw Belfast Linen (32 ct). Two strands of floss were used for Cross Stitch, 2 for candle flame Backstitch, 1 for all other Backstitch, and 1 for French Knots.

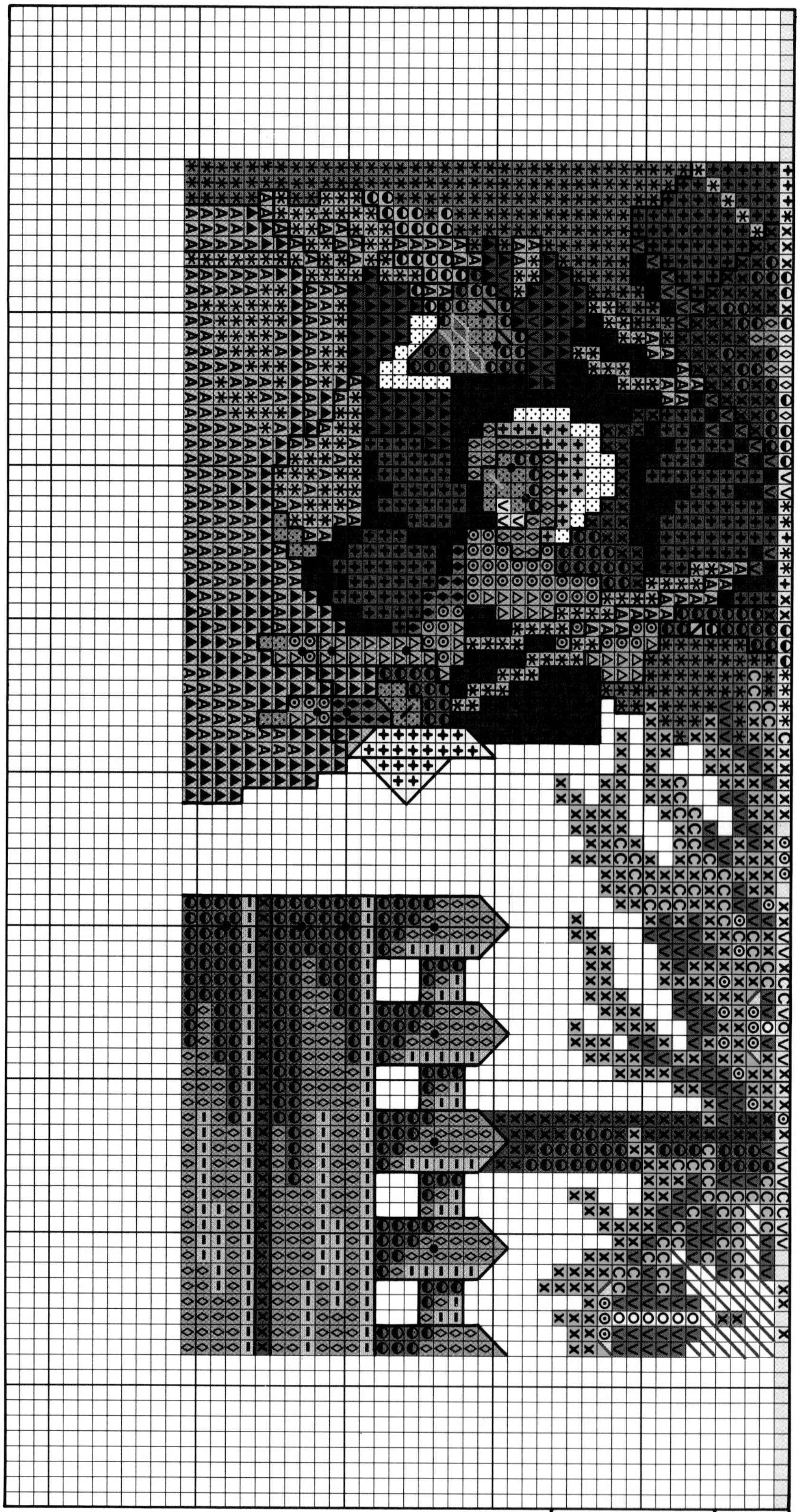

Blue area indicates last row of top section of design.

Stitch Count: 78w x 120h

Aida 11	7⅛"	x	11"
Aida 14	5⅝"	x	8⅝"
Belfast Linen 32 over 2	4⅞"	x	7½"
Aida 18	4⅜"	x	6¾"
Hardanger 22	3⅝"	x	5½"

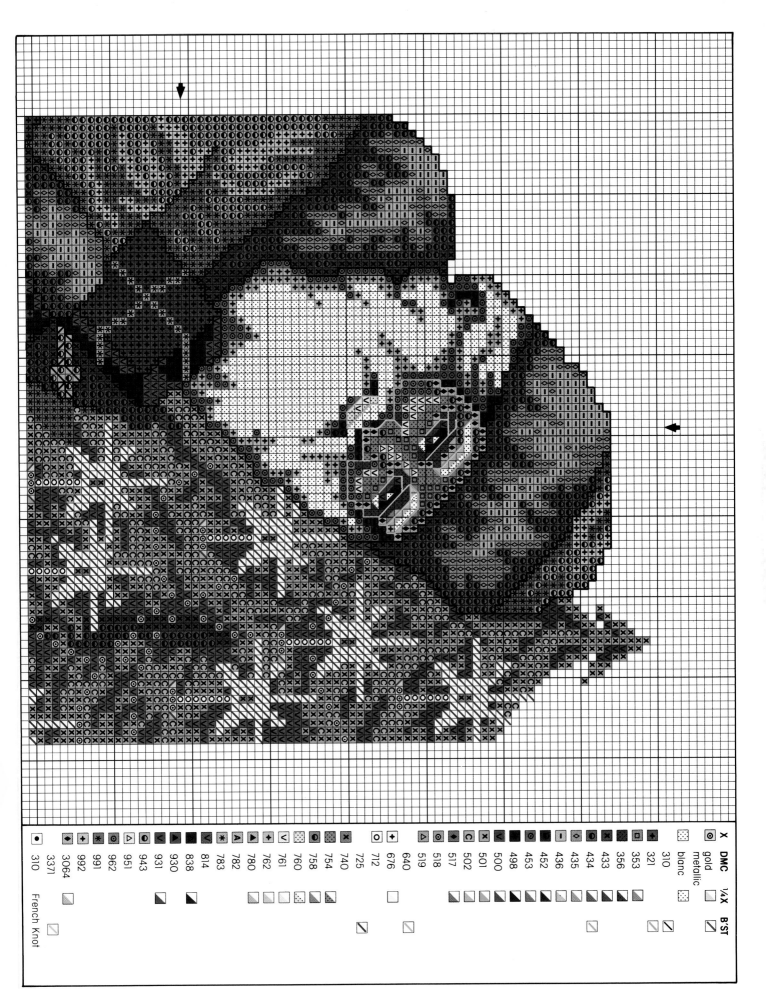

X	DMC	¼X	B'ST
⊙	gold metallic		
⊡	blanc	⊡	
	310		◥
	321		
	353	◥	
	356	◥	
	433	◥	
	434	◥	
	435	◥	
	436	◥	
	452	◥	
	453	◥	
	498	◥	
	500	◥	
	501	◥	
	502	◥	
	517	◥	◥
	518		
	519		
	640		
⊙	676		◥
⊞	712	◻	
	725		
◮	740		
◪	754	◥	
⊂	758	◥	
⊠	760	◥	
◲	761	◥	
◨	762	◥	
⊻	780		
⋇	782		
◭	783		
⊿	814	◼	
◼	838	◼	
◀	930		
⊙	931	◼	
⊛	943		
⊡	951		
⊚	962		
⊕	991		
◆	992	◻	◥
⊙	3064		
	3371		◥
●	310 French Knot	◻	

KRIS KRINGLE

Shown on page 42.

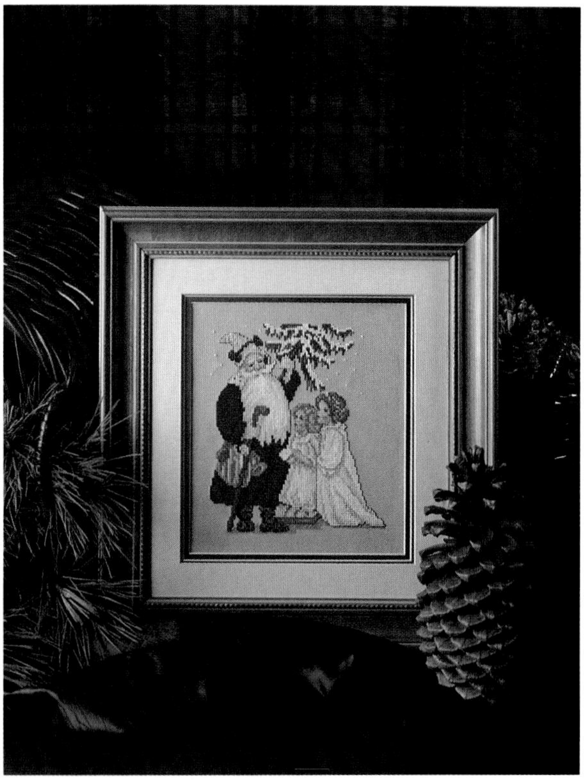

Kris Kringle was stitched over 2 fabric threads on a 15" x 16" piece of Khaki Linda (27 ct). Two strands of floss were used for Cross Stitch, 1 for Backstitch, and 1 for French Knots.

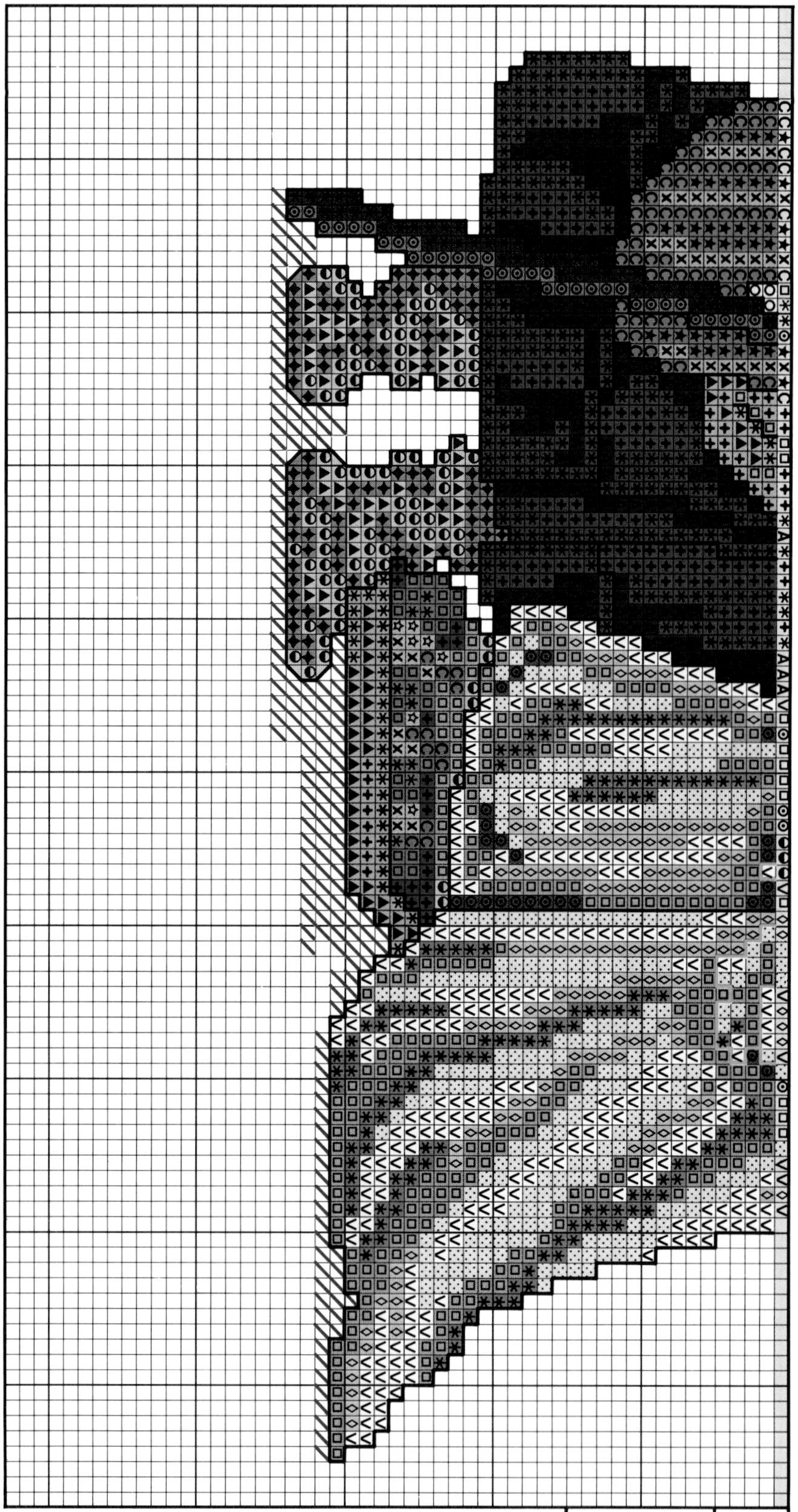

Blue area indicates last row of top section of design.

Stitch Count: 92w x 107h

Aida 11	8⅜"	x	9¾"
Linda 27 over 2	6⅞"	x	8"
Aida 14	6⅝"	x	7¾"
Aida 18	5⅛"	x	6"
Hardanger 22	4¼"	x	4⅞"

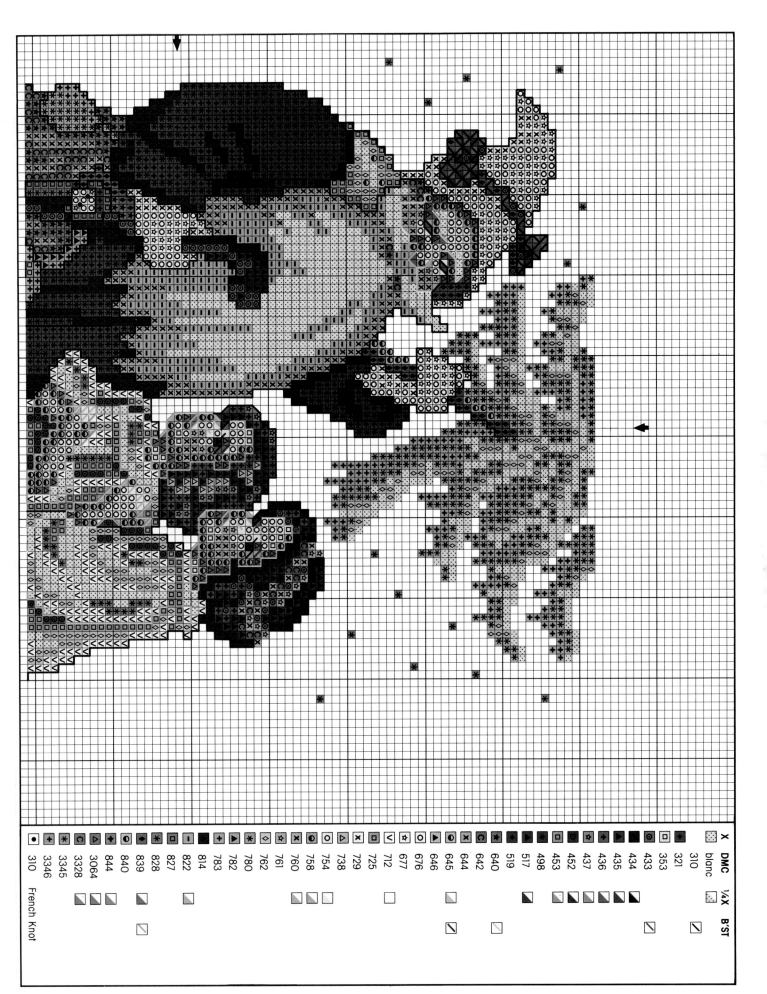

X	DMC	¼X	B'ST
▨	blanc	▨	
	310		◣
	321		
	353	▨	
	433	◣	◣
	434	◣	
	435	◣	
	436	◣	
	437	◣	
	452	◣	
	453	◣	
	498		
	517	◣	
	519		
	640		◣
	642		
	644	◣	
	645		
	646		
	676		
	677	▨	
	712		
	725		
	729		
	738		
	754	◣	
	758	◣	
	760	◣	
	761		
	762		
	780		
	782		
	783		
	814		
	822	◣	
	827		
	828		
	839		◣
	840	◣	
	844	◣	
	3064	◣	
	3328	◣	
	3345		
	3346		
	310 French Knot		

man for all seasons

Shown on page 44.

Man For All Seasons was stitched over 2 fabric threads on a 16" x 19" piece of Mushroom Lugana (25 ct). Three strands of floss were used for Cross Stitch, 4 for gold metallic Backstitch, and 1 for all other Backstitch.

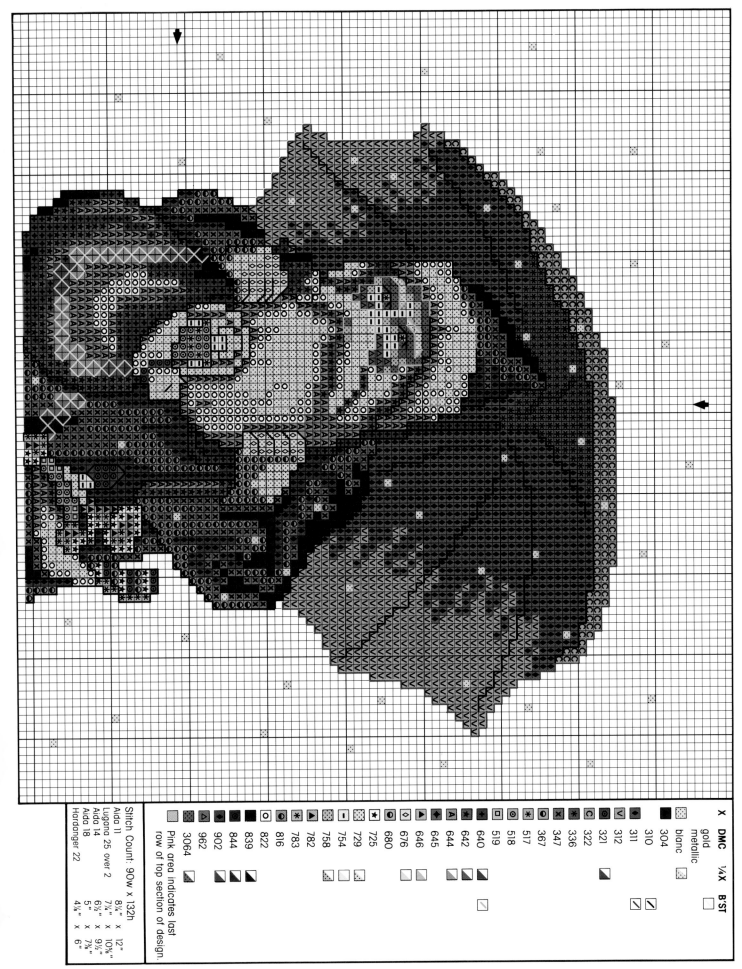

SWEET DREAMS

Shown on page 46.

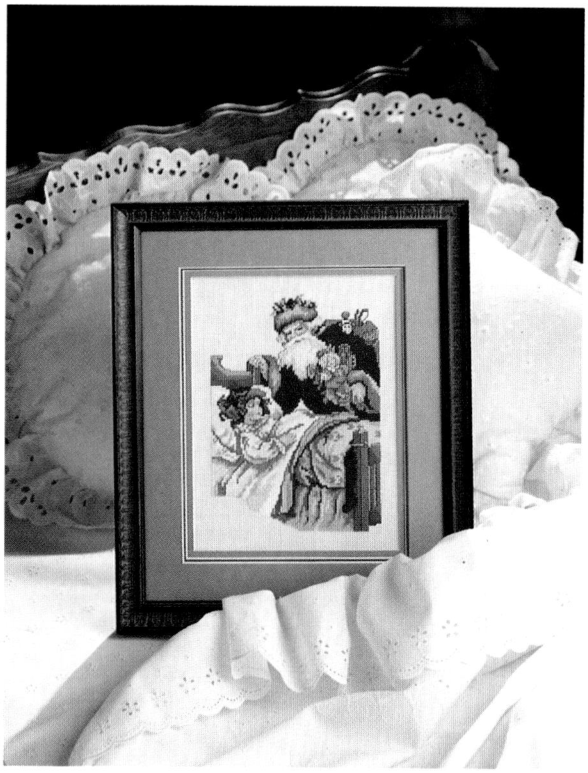

Sweet Dreams was stitched over 2 fabric threads on a 14" x 16" piece of Cream Belfast Linen (32 ct). Two strands of floss were used for Cross Stitch, 1 for Backstitch, and 2 for French Knots.

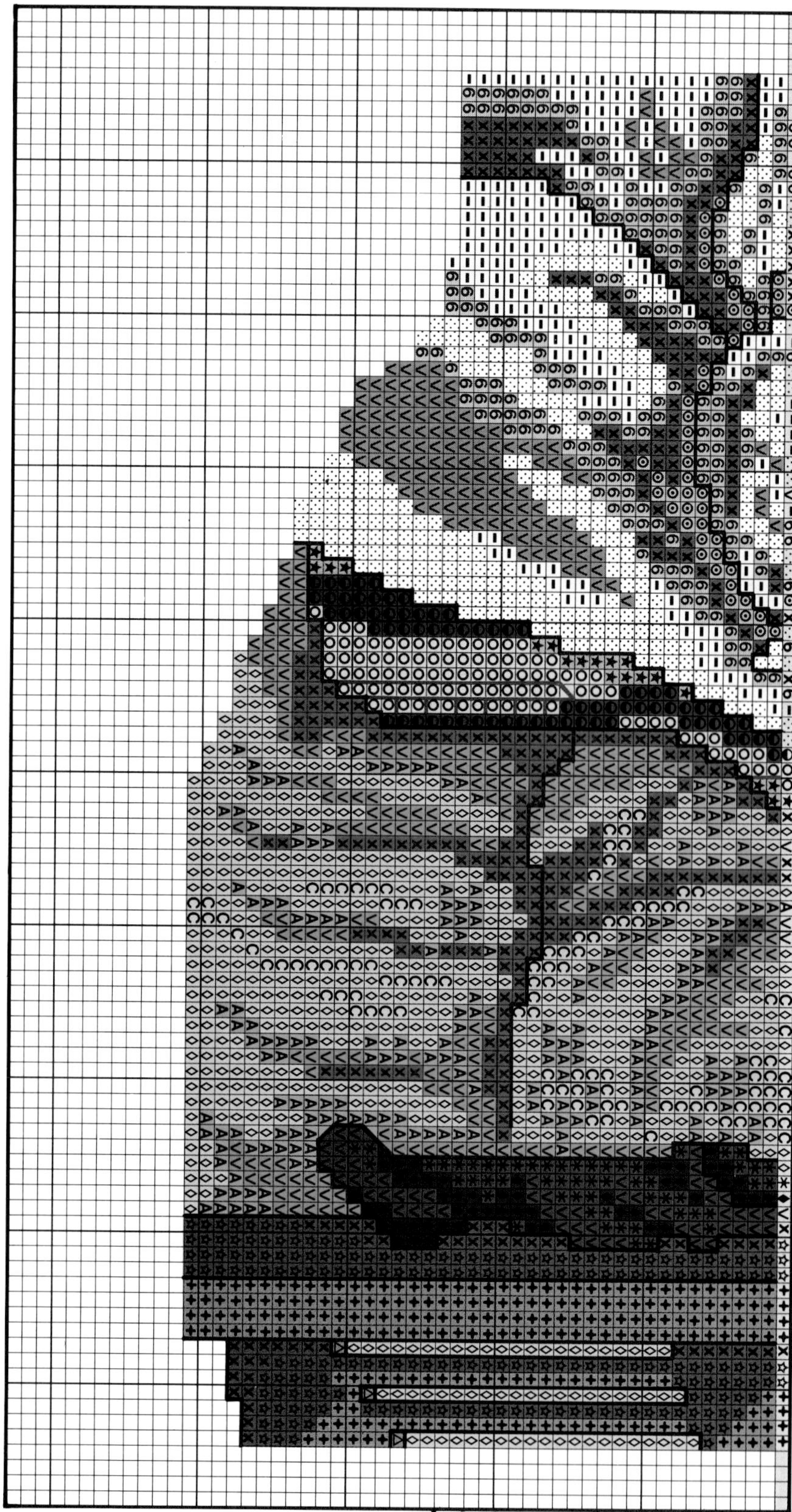

3064
3328
3371
518 French Knot
Blue area indicates last row of top section of design.

Stitch Count: 90w x 120h

Aida 11	$8\frac{1}{4}$"	x	11"
Aida 14	$6\frac{1}{2}$"	x	$8\frac{5}{8}$"
Belfast Linen 32 over 2	$5\frac{5}{8}$"	x	$7\frac{1}{2}$"
Aida 18	5"	x	$6\frac{3}{4}$"
Hardanger 22	$4\frac{1}{8}$"	x	$5\frac{1}{2}$"

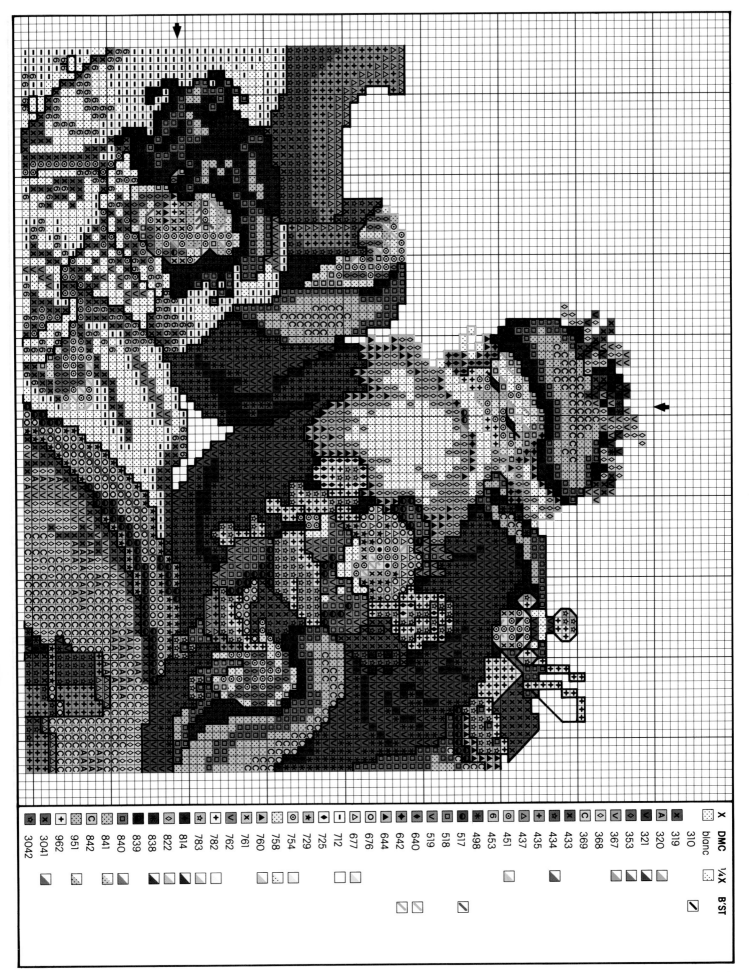

all-american santa

Shown on page 48.

All-American Santa was stitched over 2 fabric threads on a 15" x 19" piece of Pewter Lugana (25 ct). Three strands of floss were used for Cross Stitch, 1 for Backstitch, and 1 for French Knots.

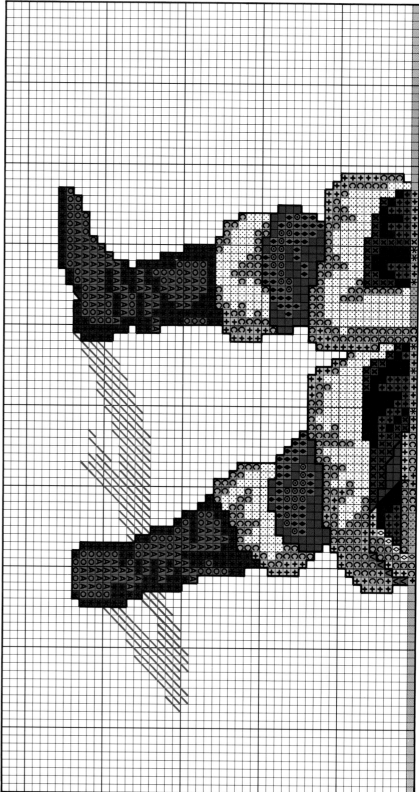

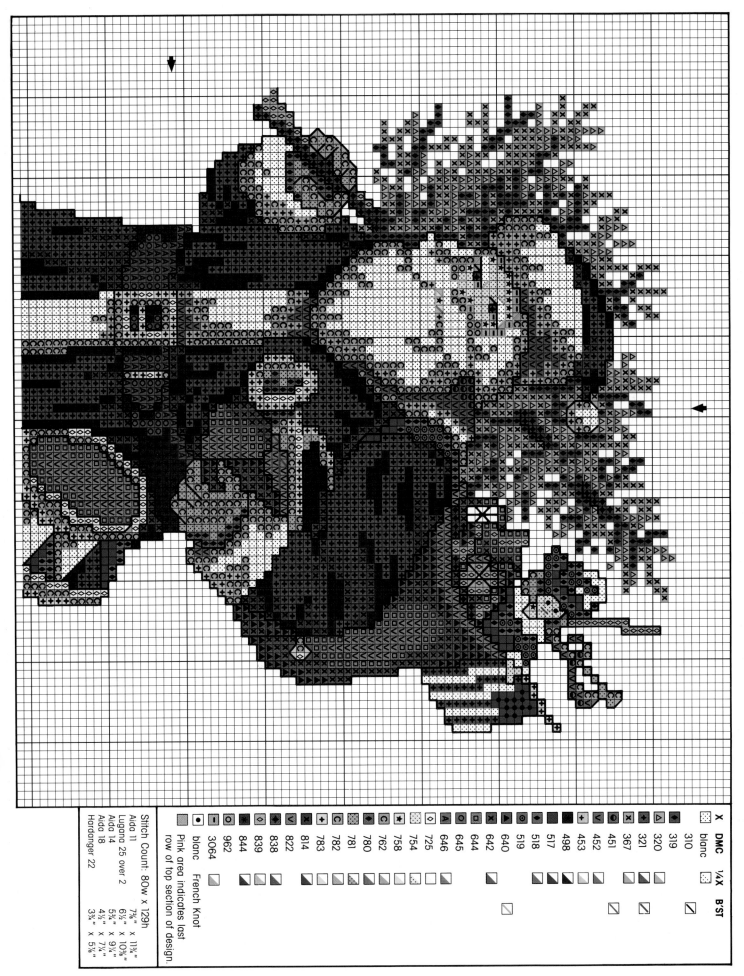

WORKING WITH CHARTS

Where To Start: The horizontal and vertical centers of each charted design are shown by arrows. You may start at any point on the charted design, but be sure the design will be centered on the fabric. Locate the center of fabric by folding in half, top to bottom and again left to right. On the charted design, count the number of squares (stitches) from the center of the chart to where you wish to start. Then from the fabric's center, find your starting point by counting out the same number of fabric threads (stitches). (**Note:** To work over two fabric threads, count out twice the number of fabric threads.)

STITCHING TIP

Working Over Two Fabric Threads: Use the sewing method instead of the stab method when working over two fabric threads. To use the sewing method, keep your stitching hand on the right side of the fabric (instead of stabbing the fabric with the needle and taking your stitching hand to the back of the fabric to pick up the needle). With the sewing method, you take the needle down and up with one stroke instead of two. To add support to the stitches, it is important that the first Cross Stitch is placed on the fabric with stitch 1-2 beginning and ending where a vertical fabric thread crosses over a horizontal fabric thread (**Fig. 1**). When the first stitch is in the correct position, the entire design will be placed properly, with vertical fabric threads supporting each stitch.

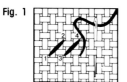

Fig. 1

STITCH DIAGRAMS

Counted Cross Stitch (X): Work one Cross Stitch to correspond to each colored square on the chart. For horizontal rows, work stitches in two journeys (**Fig. 2**). For vertical rows, complete each stitch as shown (**Fig. 3**). When the chart shows a Backstitch crossing a colored square (**Fig. 4**), a Cross Stitch (**Fig. 2 or 3**) should be worked first; then the Backstitch (**Fig. 7**) should be worked on top of the Cross Stitch.

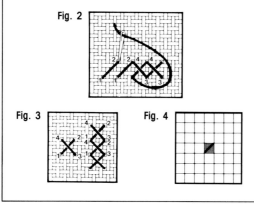

Fig. 2

Fig. 3   **Fig. 4**

Half Cross Stitch (½X): This stitch is one journey of the Cross Stitch and is worked from lower left to upper right as shown in **Fig. 5**.

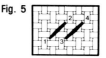

Fig. 5

Quarter Stitch (¼X): Quarter Stitches are denoted by triangular shapes of color on the chart and on the color key. Come up at 1; then go down at 2 (**Fig. 6**).

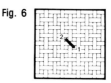

Fig. 6

Backstitch (B'ST): For outline detail, Backstitch (shown on chart and on color key by black or colored straight lines) should be worked after the design has been completed (**Fig. 7**).

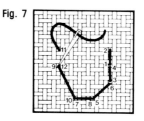

Fig. 7

French Knot: Bring needle up at 1. Wrap thread once around needle and insert needle at 2, holding end of thread with non-stitching fingers (**Fig. 8**). Tighten knot; then pull needle through fabric, holding thread until it must be released. For larger knot, use more strands; wrap only once.

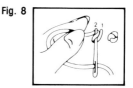

Fig. 8

Designs stitched by Andrea Ahlen, Janet Baker, Caren Beard, Vicky Bishop, Kim Camp, Trudi Drinkwater, Miriam Durrett, Kathy Elrod, Gail Fry, Dawn Hatfield, Catherine Hubmann, Phyllis Lundy, Jerri Miller, Ray Ellen Odle, Debbie Painter, Linda Pemberton, Mary Anna Phinney, Sandy Pigue, Karen Sisco, Susan Sullivan, Patricia Vines, and Marie Williford.

The Night Before Christmas

Twas the night before Christmas, when all through the house Not a creature was stirring, not even a mouse; The stockings were hung by the chimney with care, In hopes that St. Nicholas soon would be there; The children were nestled all snug in their beds, While visions of sugar-plums danced through their heads; And mamma in her kerchief, and I in my cap, Had just settled our brains for a long winter's nap, — When out on the lawn there arose such a clatter, I sprang from my bed to see what was the matter. Away to the window I flew like a flash, Tore open the shutters and threw up the sash. The moon, on the breast of the new-fallen snow, Gave a lustre of midday to objects below; When what to my wondering eyes should appear, But a miniature sleigh and eight tiny reindeer, With a little old driver, so lively and quick I knew in a moment it must be St. Nick. More rapid than eagles his coursers they came, And he whistled and shouted and called them by name: "Now, Dasher! now, Dancer! now, Prancer and Vixen! On, Comet! on, Cupid! on, Donder and Blitzen! To the top of the porch, to the top of the wall! Now, dash away, dash away, dash away all!" As dry leaves that before the wild hurricane fly, When they meet with an obstacle, mount to the sky, So, up to the house-top the coursers they flew, With a sleigh full of toys, — and St. Nicholas too. And then in a twinkling I heard on the roof The prancing and pawing of each little hoof. As I drew in my head and was turning around, Down the chimney St. Nicholas came with a bound. He was dressed all in fur from his head to his foot, And his clothes were all tarnished with ashes and soot; A bundle of toys he had flung on his back, And he looked like a peddler just opening his pack. His eyes how they twinkled! his dimples how merry! His cheeks were like roses, his nose like a cherry; His droll little mouth was drawn up like a bow, And the beard on his chin was as white as the snow. The stump of a pipe he held tight in his teeth, And the smoke it encircled his head like a wreath. He had a broad face, and a little round belly That shook, when he laughed, like a bowl full of jelly. He was chubby and plump, — a right jolly old elf — And I laughed when I saw him, in spite of myself. A wink of his eye and a twist of his head Soon gave me to know I had nothing to dread. He spoke not a word, but went straight to his work, And filled all the stockings; then turned with a jerk, And laying his finger aside of his nose, And giving a nod, up the chimney he rose. He sprang to his sleigh, to his team gave a whistle, And away they all flew like the down of a thistle; But I heard him exclaim, ere he drove out of sight: "Happy Christmas to all, and to all a good-night!"

— Clement Clarke Moore

DMC	COLOR	ANC.	DMC	COLOR	ANC.	DMC	COLOR	ANC.
blanc	white	02	519	lt blue	0167	842	vy lt beige brown	0376
ecru	ecru	0387	561	vy dk aqua	0212	844	vy dk grey	0401
223	shell pink	0895	597	dk turquoise	0168	869	dk yellow beige	0889
224	lt shell pink	0894	598	turquoise	0928	890	dk forest green	0218
300	vy dk copper	0352	610	dk taupe	0905	892	dk carnation pink	029
301	dk copper	0351	611	taupe	0898	893	carnation pink	028
304	red	047	612	lt taupe	0832	894	lt carnation pink	026
309	dk rose	042	632	vy dk flesh	0352	895	forest green	0218
310	black	0403	640	dk beige	0393	899	dk pink	026
311	navy blue	0149	642	beige	0392	900	vy dk orange	0334
312	lt navy blue	0979	644	lt beige	0391	902	dk maroon	0897
315	dk mauve	0972	645	dk grey	0400	918	dk rust	0341
316	mauve	0969	646	grey	8581	922	copper	0349
317	steel grey	0400	647	lt grey	0900	924	dk blue green	0851
319	vy dk green	0217	648	vy lt grey	0847	926	blue green	0850
320	green	0215	666	vy lt red	046	927	lt blue green	0849
321	lt red	019	676	lt gold	0891	928	vy lt blue green	0848
322	vy lt navy blue	0978	677	vy lt gold	0292	930	dk grey blue	0922
326	vy dk rose	059	680	dk gold	0901	931	grey blue	0921
327	dk violet	0100	712	cream	0926	932	lt grey blue	0920
335	rose	041	720	orange	0326	935	dk khaki green	0846
336	dk navy blue	0150	725	dk yellow	0297	937	vy dk yellow green	0269
341	lt periwinkle blue	0939	726	yellow	0305	938	dk brown	0380
347	vy dk salmon	013	727	lt yellow	0293	943	aqua	0189
349	dk coral	046	729	gold	0890	946	dk orange	0332
350	coral	011	738	lt tan	0367	948	vy lt flesh	0892
351	lt coral	010	739	vy lt tan	0366	951	vy lt copper	0880
353	vy lt coral	08	740	vy lt orange	0316	962	vy dk pink	027
355	rust	5968	746	vy lt yellow	0386	963	vy lt pink	023
356	lt rust	5975	747	lt turquoise	0158	970	lt orange	0925
367	dk green	0216	754	lt flesh	4146	991	dk aqua	0211
368	lt green	0214	758	vy lt rust	9575	992	lt aqua	0187
369	vy lt green	0213	760	salmon	09	993	vy lt aqua	0186
402	lt copper	0347	761	lt salmon	08	3011	khaki green	0845
407	flesh	0914	762	vy lt steel grey	0397	3012	lt khaki green	0844
413	dk steel grey	0401	772	vy lt olive green	0259	3013	vy lt khaki green	0843
415	lt steel grey	0398	775	lt sky blue	0128	3021	grey brown	0905
420	yellow beige	0906	776	lt pink	024	3041	violet	0871
422	vy lt yellow beige	0887	778	lt mauve	0968	3042	lt violet	0870
433	lt brown	0358	780	vy dk topaz	0309	3045	lt yellow beige	0888
434	vy lt brown	0310	781	dk topaz	0308	3064	dk flesh	0883
435	vy dk tan	0365	782	topaz	0307	3326	pink	025
436	dk tan	0363	783	lt topaz	0306	3328	dk salmon	011
437	tan	0362	792	dk periwinkle blue	0941	3345	vy dk olive green	0269
451	dk shell grey	8581	793	periwinkle blue	0940	3346	dk olive green	0268
452	shell grey	0900	801	brown	0359	3347	olive green	0266
453	lt shell grey	0847	814	maroon	044	3348	lt olive green	0265
469	dk yellow green	0268	815	lt maroon	022	3371	vy dk brown	0382
470	yellow green	0267	816	vy dk red	043			
471	lt yellow green	0266	817	vy dk coral	013			
472	vy lt yellow green	0253	822	vy lt beige	0390			
498	dk red	043	823	vy dk navy blue	0152			
500	dk grey green	0879	827	sky blue	0976			
501	grey green	0878	828	vy lt blue	0158			
502	lt grey green	0876	838	vy dk beige brown	0360			
503	vy lt grey green	0875	839	dk beige brown	0936			
517	dk blue	0169	840	beige brown	0379			
518	blue	0168	841	lt beige brown	0378			

We have made every effort to ensure that these instructions are accurate and complete. We cannot, however, be responsible for human error, typographical mistakes, or variations in individual work.

CREATE A CHRISTMAS YOU'LL ALWAYS REMEMBER...

LEISURE ARTS PRESENTS
THE SPIRIT OF CHRISTMAS
CREATIVE HOLIDAY IDEAS
BOOK THREE

With our annual book, *The Spirit of Christmas*, you can create memorable decorations, unforgettable gifts, and delicious holiday foods. Within the 160 pages of the 1989 edition, you'll find more than 200 all-new projects and recipes to enhance the holidays for you and your loved ones. Exquisite, full-color photographs and clear, easy-to-follow instructions accompany each project. You'll come back to this unique volume time and time again!

TO ORDER BY PHONE:
CALL TOLL FREE
1-800-666-6326

7 a.m. to 9 p.m. Monday-Friday
7 a.m. to 3 p.m. Saturday (CST)

ALSO AVAILABLE AT YOUR NEEDLECRAFT SHOP!

FREE FOR 21 DAYS!

To review *The Spirit of Christmas* free in your home for 21 days, call the toll free number on this page or write to Leisure Arts, Dept. 69SR, P.O. Box 10576, Des Moines, IA 50340-0576. If you like our book, pay just $18.95 (in U.S. funds), plus $1.95 postage and handling. If not completely delighted, you may return the book within 21 days and owe nothing. If you keep it, we will automatically send you each new Christmas annual, on approval, as it is published. You are in no way obligated to buy any future annuals, and you may cancel at any time just by notifying us.

Please allow 4-6 weeks for delivery.   Limited Time Offer